HIGH-FLAVOR,
LOW-FAT
APPETIZERS

Steven Raichlen's

HIGH-FLAVOR, LOW-FAT APPETIZERS

Photography by Greg Schneider

VIKING

VIKING
Published by the Penguin Group
Penguin Books USA Inc., 375 Hudson Street,
New York, New York 10014, U.S.A.
Penguin Books Ltd, 27 Wrights Lane,
London W8 5TZ, England
Penguin Books Australia Ltd, Ringwood,
Victoria, Australia
Penguin Books Canada Ltd, 10 Alcorn Avenue,
Toronto, Ontario, Canada M4V 3B2
Penguin Books (N.Z.) Ltd, 182–190 Wairau Road,
Auckland 10, New Zealand

Penguin Books Ltd, Registered Offices:
Harmondsworth, Middlesex, England

First published in 1997 by Viking Penguin,
a division of Penguin Books USA Inc.

1 3 5 7 9 10 8 6 4 2

Copyright © Steven Raichlen, 1997
Photographs copyright © Greg Schneider, 1997
All rights reserved

LIBRARY OF CONGRESS CATALOGING-IN-PUBLICATION DATA
Raichlen, Steven.
[High-flavor, low-fat appetizers]
Steven Raichlen's high-flavor, low-fat appetizers.
p.   cm.
Includes index.
ISBN 0-670-87135-4
1. Appetizers.   2. Low-fat diet—Recipes.   3. Cookery,
International.   I. Title.
TX740.R32   1997
641.8'12—dc20   96-19369

This book is printed on acid-free paper.

∞

Printed in the United States of America
Set in Goudy

To Katherine Kenny
and twenty years of friendship

ACKNOWLEDGMENTS

This may be a little book, but it took a lot of work on the part of many people.

First, I want to thank my recipe testers: Elida Proenza, Cathy Peplowski, Kevin Pierce, and Magda Queimado. We mourn Magda's tragic death and will sorely miss her. Her spirit lives on in her lovely daughter, Mariana.

Greg Schneider has again brought my recipes to life with his stunning photographs and irrepressible spirit. He was assisted by the ever-cheerful Michael Donnelly. Debbie Cheleotis provided logistical support in the office. Karen Brasel did the nutritional analyses. My cousin Stephanie Aronson makes her debut as a professional potter with the plate featured on page 36. And a big thanks to my friends at Scotty's market.

Dawn Drzal at Viking Penguin graced the manuscript with her expert editing. I'd like to thank all my friends at Viking for their enthusiasm and support, including Barbara Grossman, Cathy Hemming, Norm Sheinman, Paul Slovak, Patti Kelly, and Elizabeth Riley.

Above all, I want to thank my family, especially the children—Jake, Betsy, and Mark—who showed remarkable forbearance when it came to not eating the food destined for photography. And, of course, my wife, Barbara, who survived yet another photo shoot and whose love and support make this—and all my books—possible.

PHOTO CREDITS

My heartfelt thanks to the following for providing props and accessories:

Delores "DJ" Sticht and Dusty Weiss, of Burdines.

Yvette Kalinowsky, of Iberia Tiles.

Stephanie Aronson, potter.

Manuel Ruvuelta, artist.

CONTENTS

INTRODUCTION

Remember the cocktail party? That high-calorie array of fat-laden fritters, artery-clogging dips, and butter-drenched canapés? If ever a meal was a minefield for health-minded eaters, it was surely the traditional party spread. Fortunately, times have changed. And so have appetites. Today, a more health-conscious approach governs party menu planning and hors d'oeuvre spreads.

The appetizers of today are high in flavor, low in fat, and international in inspiration. Nutrition-minded eaters are discovering a bold new world of flavors: quesadillas from Mexico; bruschette from Italy; satés from Southeast Asia. "Shop and cook locally, but menu-plan globally" has become the battle cry of the modern cook.

For that matter, our whole attitude toward finger fare has changed. Once considered an adjunct to a meal, appetizers are more and more becoming a meal in themselves. Call it grazing—or tapas or dim sum. More and more health-conscious Americans are serving a variety of appetizers and starters not just as a prelude to a meal but as the main course. This is my favorite way of eating. I love the diversity of a meal of starters—the wonderful contrast of textures, tastes, and shapes.

This book was inspired in part by a friend, Miami journalist Jane Wooldridge. An avid party giver, gracious hostess, and enthusiastic supporter of the High-Flavor, Low-Fat philosophy, Jane has urged me for several years to write a High-Flavor, Low-Fat appetizer book. There's a reason for her persistence: while most of us have adopted a healthier, low-fat diet for our everyday meals, we all too often subject our family and friends to a fat assault when we entertain.

Fortunately, it's easy to create appetizers and party fare that are high in flavor and low in fat. The cream- and butter-based dips of yesteryear are being replaced with silky purées of beans and other vegetables. Chips have shed their fat by being baked instead of deep-fried. The advent of no-fat sour cream and yogurt have given blintzes and cream sauces a new life. New cooking techniques such as "oven frying" make it possible to serve crackling-crisp empanadas and other savory pastries with greatly reduced fat. Even vegetable sticks have been given new-found nobility: we now honor them with their French name, *crudités*.

SOME TECHNIQUES FOR TRIMMING THE FAT FROM PARTY FARE

Readers of my previous High-Flavor, Low-Fat books will recognize many of the techniques I use in this book to create bold flavors with little or no fat. One is a generous use of herbs and spices to replace the richness once achieved with animal fats. Another is the use of chicken or vegetable stock instead of oil or butter to create moist, creamy dips and spreads.

Here are some other techniques that can be used in preparing High-Flavor, Low-Fat party fare.

- Yogurt cheese and low- and no-fat cottage cheese and cream cheese are great for making dairy-based dips and spreads. If your fat budget allows it, use the low-fat product: it has much more flavor than the no-fat version. But nonfat dairy products can produce some very fine food, too. For a richer, creamier texture, drain the yogurt or cottage cheese in a yogurt strainer (or a cheesecloth-lined strainer) before using. Yogurt can be drained in as little as 4 hours, but the resulting yogurt cheese will be firmer and drier if you start the previous night.

- Egg whites have the same jelling and leavening properties as whole eggs, without the fat of the yolk. Thus, I use them in a variety of dishes, from fillings to custards to cheesecakes. Egg whites are the active ingredient in such egg substitutes as Egg Beaters. I consider myself a purist, so you might be surprised to find recipes in this book that call for egg substitutes. The reason is simple: egg substitutes are more than 95 percent egg whites, and there's no appreciable difference in taste.

- Everyone loves crisp finger food at cocktail parties—but not the fat associated with deep frying. While working on this book, I discovered that wonton skins and ravioli wrappers could be baked instead of deep-fried. The result is a crackling-crisp crust with very little fat. And Asian wrappers are a lot quicker and easier to use than filo dough. I call this method of cooking "oven frying."

- Garlic, spices, and chili peppers are a great way to achieve flavor without fat. I have a rather high tolerance for intense flavors and chili hellfire. I've tried to suggest a range of these ingredients for people who may have more timid palates. Start with the minimum quantity of these flavorings and add more as needed.

SOME GENERAL OBSERVATIONS ON PARTY PLANNING

The French term *hors d'oeuvre* literally means "outside the main work." But there's no reason to dismiss this, the most diverse branch of cooking, as secondary or unessential. Although great hors d'oeuvres can't guarantee a great party, it's harder to have one without them. Besides, interesting party fare certainly gives people something to talk about.

Choose dishes that can be prepared ahead of time and served at room temperature, or those that can be cooked or warmed at the last minute. Your place as host is with your guests, not in the kitchen.

Keep the menu as interesting as the conversation. Balance hot and cold, soft and crunchy, Eastern and Western. Whether you plan to serve 4 items or 14, offer a variety of flavors, textures, and temperatures. I like to balance hot offerings, like dumplings and quesadillas, with cold ones, like dips based on yogurt or sour cream. Soft, creamy spreads make a nice contrast to crunchy pastries and vegetable sticks.

When it comes to planning a party spread, remember that good things come in small packages. Small means bite-size hors d'oeuvres that can be popped into the mouth without interrupting the conversation. For the convenience of your guests and the cleanliness of your carpets, make sure that passed fare can be consumed in one or two bites. Otherwise, provide plates and cutlery.

Avoid traffic jams. Your menu should include stationary fare, like dips, chips, and vegetable sticks, as well as passed items, such as kebabs and pastries. Have the food dispersed throughout the party area so your guests can enjoy it without getting stuck in bottlenecks.

Reduce your anxiety by having enough food. How much is enough depends on the time of your party and the kind of crowd you expect.

In this book I have not always specified the number of servings in a recipe; instead, I have given the number of pieces a particular recipe will yield. Figure on 6 to 8 pieces of mixed or single hors d'oeuvres to serve one person as an appetizer; or at a party with dinner to follow, 10 to 12 pieces when the hors d'oeuvres are the only food in sight for hours. Add 2 to 3 more pieces if the crowd likes to drink.

All the recipes in this book can be multiplied to serve large numbers of people.

BASIC PROCEDURES

Two procedures are called for again and again in this book: peeling and seeding tomatoes, and draining yogurt to make yogurt cheese. For the sake of conciseness, I describe the procedures in full here.

To Peel a Tomato

Method one: Using the tip of a paring knife, cut the stem end out of the tomato and cut a shallow X in the rounded end. Plunge the tomato in rapidly boiling water for 15 to 60 seconds. (The riper the tomato, the shorter the cooking time required.) Rinse the tomato under cold water or let cool on a plate until you can comfortably handle it, then pull off the skin with your fingers. It will slip off in broad strips.

Method two: This method has the added advantage of producing a decorative tomato rose.

Starting from the bottom (the end opposite the stem) and using a sharp paring knife, pare off the skin in a single continuous strip, ¾ to 1 inch wide, the way Meg Ryan peeled an apple in the movie *Sleepless in Seattle*. To make a tomato rose, roll up the strip as you would a sheet of paper. Set the roll on end: it will look like a rose.

To Seed a Tomato

Cut the tomato in half crosswise and squeeze each half in the palm of your hand, cut side down, to wring out the seeds and liquid. Work over a bowl and strainer. Push the pulp through the strainer with the back of a spoon. Reserve the tomato liquid that collects in the bowl for sauces, soups, or even drinking.

One peeled, seeded medium tomato produces about ¾ cup chopped.

To Make Yogurt Cheese

Place 1 quart nonfat plain yogurt in a yogurt strainer or regular strainer lined with cheesecloth or paper towels. Place the strainer over a bowl in the refrigerator. Let the yogurt drain for at least 4 hours, preferably overnight. Four hours will give you soft curds; overnight, firm curds.

Makes about 1¾ cups yogurt cheese.

ONE FINAL NOTE

Finally, please note that the philosophy I espouse is low-fat, not fat-free, cooking. I'd rather use a little fat to make great-tasting hors d'oeuvres than no fat to make fare that tastes more like medicine than party food. Many of my recipes will call for a range of fat: 1 to 2 tablespoons oil, 1 to 2 eggs, and so on. Choose the option that best fits your fat budget and overall calorie allowance.

That being said, I have tried to remain within contemporary nutritional guidelines, offering food that is low in total fat, saturated fat, and the proportion of calories derived from fat. When a range of yields is given, the nutritional analysis is based on the lower yield.

Remember: food isn't poison. The occasional splurge won't kill you. Julia Child preaches moderation in all things, especially in eating. We should all live as long and productive a life as she has.

DIPS, CHIPS, AND VEGETABLE STICKS

MESS O' CHIPS

Remember chips? That tasty but oh-so-unhealthy snack made by deep-frying wedges of fresh tortilla? Baking produces an equally crisp chip without the fat. When making a batch of chips, I like to use white (wheat-flour), yellow-corn, and blue-corn tortillas to wind up with a colorful assortment. (Blue-corn tortillas are available at natural foods stores, gourmet shops, and Hispanic and Southwestern grocery stores.) But any sort of tortilla will do.

2 yellow-corn tortillas
2 blue-corn tortillas

2 flour tortillas

1. Preheat the oven to 350° F. Cut each tortilla into 8 wedges (10 to 12 wedges for large flour tortillas). Arrange the wedges in a single layer on nonstick baking sheets.

2. Bake the chips until lightly browned and crisp, about 10 minutes. Be especially careful with the flour tortillas, as they burn easily. Transfer the chips to a cooling rack.

Makes 48 to 72 chips, which will serve 8 to 10

6 CALORIES PER SERVING; 0.2 G PROTEIN; 0.1 G FAT; 0 G SATURATED FAT; 1 G CARBOHYDRATE; 6 MG SODIUM; 0 MG CHOLESTEROL

Mess o' Chips
A New Guacamole
Savannah Salsa
Mango Salsa

A NEW GUACAMOLE

Guacamole is probably the most popular dip in the country. Unfortunately, the main ingredient, avocado, is quite high in fat. This version cuts the fat by replacing a portion of the avocado with green peas. Believe me, it tastes better than it sounds.

1 small ripe avocado, peeled and pitted
1 cup cooked green peas, cooking liquid
  reserved
1 to 2 cloves garlic, peeled
4 scallions, trimmed and coarsely chopped
1 to 2 jalapeño chilies, seeded and coarsely
  chopped (for a spicier guacamole, leave in
  the seeds)

¼ cup chopped fresh cilantro, plus sprigs for
  garnish
Salt and freshly ground black pepper
3 to 4 tablespoons fresh lime juice, or to taste
3 to 4 tablespoons chicken stock, vegetable
  stock, or pea cooking liquid
1 ripe tomato, seeded and diced (optional)
  (see page xiv)

1. Purée the avocado, peas, garlic, scallions, chilies, and cilantro in a food processor and season with salt and pepper. Gradually add the lime juice and enough stock or pea cooking liquid to obtain a creamy, smooth purée. Stir in the tomato, if using. Correct the seasoning with lime juice and salt: the guacamole should be highly seasoned.

2. Transfer the guacamole to a serving bowl and garnish with the cilantro sprigs. Serve with Mess o' Chips (see page 1).

Makes 2½ to 3 cups, which will serve 8 to 12

63 CALORIES PER SERVING; 1.8 G PROTEIN; 3.4 G FAT; 0.7 G SATURATED FAT; 7 G CARBOHYDRATE; 55 MG SODIUM; 0 MG CHOLESTEROL

SAVANNAH SALSA

I love the nutty, earthy flavor of black-eyed peas. But until recently, this distinctive legume was enjoyed primarily in the South, where it is an essential ingredient in the classic Southern New Year's Day dish, hoppin' John. Contemporary American chefs have given black-eyed peas a newfound respectability. I like to use a mix of red, green, and yellow bell peppers in this salsa, but any color will do.

2 cups cooked black-eyed peas (see Note)
1 bell pepper, cut into ¼-inch dice
  (about 1 cup)
½ small red onion, cut into ¼-inch dice
1 stalk celery, cut into ¼-inch dice
1 clove garlic, minced
1 to 2 jalapeño chilies, minced (for a spicier
  salsa, leave in the seeds)

½ cup chopped fresh parsley (preferably flat-
  leaf), plus sprig for garnish
3 tablespoons red-wine vinegar, or to taste
2 tablespoons extra-virgin olive oil
Salt and freshly ground black pepper

1. Put the peas, bell peppers, onion, celery, garlic, jalapeño, parsley, vinegar, and oil in a nonreactive mixing bowl. Season with salt and pepper, and toss to combine. Correct the seasoning with salt, pepper, and vinegar: the salsa should be highly seasoned.

2. Transfer the salsa to a serving bowl and garnish with the parsley sprig. Serve with Mess o' Chips (see page 1).

Note: Instructions for cooking black-eyed peas from scratch can be found in my book *High-Flavor, Low-Fat Vegetarian Cooking*. You can certainly use canned beans for this recipe (try to pick a low-sodium brand, which you will find in a natural foods store). If you use canned beans, rinse them thoroughly with cold water and drain well.

Makes 3 cups, which will serve 10 to 12

68 CALORIES PER SERVING; 3 G PROTEIN; 3 G FAT; 0.5 G SATURATED FAT; 9 G CARBOHYDRATE; 48 MG SODIUM; 0 MG CHOLESTEROL

MANGO SALSA

If the 1970s were the kiwi decade and the 1980s the raspberry decade, then the 1990s will surely be remembered as the decade we discovered mangoes. Once the province of Floridian cooks, this oval, orange-fleshed fruit with its peachy-pineappley flavor has taken the nation by storm. When you buy mangoes, look for heavy, unblemished fruits. Let them ripen at room temperature until squeezably soft and very fragrant. Some, but not all, varieties turn red when ripe, so you really need to judge ripeness by smell and touch. This salsa is also delicious made with other fruits, such as peaches, pineapple, or melon.

2 to 3 ripe mangoes
1 cucumber, peeled, seeded, and cut into
   ¼-inch dice (see Note)
4 large or 8 small scallions, trimmed and
   finely chopped (about ½ cup)
½ red bell pepper, cut into ¼-inch dice
1 tablespoon minced candied ginger or fresh
   ginger

½ to 1 Scotch bonnet, habanero, or other hot
   chili, minced
¼ cup chopped fresh mint or cilantro
3 tablespoons rice vinegar or fresh lime juice,
   or to taste
2 tablespoons packed light-brown sugar,
   or to taste
Salt and freshly ground black pepper

1. Peel the mangoes and cut the flesh off the pits. Cut the flesh into ¼-inch dice: you should have about 1½ cups.

2. Put the mango, cucumber, scallion, bell pepper, ginger, chili pepper, mint, vinegar, and sugar in a nonreactive mixing bowl, season with salt and pepper, and toss to combine. Correct the seasoning with vinegar and sugar: the salsa should be a little tart, a little sweet, and very highly seasoned. You can prepare the ingredients ahead of time, but don't mix them more than 20 minutes before serving. Serve with Mess o' Chips (see page 1).

Note: To seed cucumbers, cut them in half lengthwise and scrape out the seeds with a melon baller or spoon.

Makes about 3 cups, which will serve 10 to 12

45 CALORIES PER SERVING; 0.6 G PROTEIN; 0.2 G FAT; 0 G SATURATED FAT; 11 G CARBOHYDRATE; 3 MG SODIUM; 0 MG CHOLESTEROL

THREE-TOMATO SALSA

Here's a colorful salsa that takes advantage of some of the exotic new tomato varieties turning up at gourmet shops. Technically speaking, tomatillos aren't tomatoes (they are related to the ground cherry), but they look like green cherry tomatoes encased in a loose papery skin and taste like tart green tomatoes. Don't worry if you can't find tomatillos or yellow tomatoes: ripe red tomatoes will make a perfectly luscious salsa. (You'll need about 2 cups diced tomatoes in all.) I've given a range of chilies: by now I'm sure you know that I like my food hot!

1 ripe red tomato, seeded and cut into ¼-inch dice (see page xiv)
1 ripe yellow tomato, seeded and cut into ¼-inch dice
4 to 6 tomatillos, cut into ¼-inch dice
½ red onion, finely chopped

1 to 4 jalapeño chilies, seeded and finely chopped (for a spicier salsa, leave in the seeds)
¼ cup chopped fresh cilantro
3 to 4 tablespoons fresh lime juice, or to taste
Salt and freshly ground black pepper

Put the tomatoes, tomatillo, onion, jalapeño, cilantro, and lime juice in a nonreactive mixing bowl, season with salt and pepper, and toss to combine. Correct the seasoning with salt and lime juice: the salsa should be highly seasoned. Serve with Mess o' Chips (see page 1).

Note: You can prepare the ingredients ahead of time, but don't mix them more than 20 minutes before serving.

Makes about 2 cups, which will serve 6 to 8

26 CALORIES PER SERVING; 0.9 G PROTEIN; 0.4 G FAT; 0 G SATURATED FAT; 6 G CARBOHYDRATE; 5 MG SODIUM; 0 MG CHOLESTEROL

VEGETABLE STICKS WITH DRY DIPS

Dry dips make a nice switch from the usual sour cream- and yogurt-based concoctions found on most buffet spreads. Dry dips are nothing more than spice mixes, and they adhere nicely to moist vegetables such as cucumber, pepper, and zucchini spears. Here are four of my favorites. Feel free to use vegetables other than the ones called for below. Note: Although I've given salt in the amounts I would use, I've added the words "or to taste," since many people like to restrict the salt in their diet.

4 stalks celery
2 zucchini
1 cucumber, peeled and seeded
  (see Note on page 4)

1 red bell pepper
1 yellow bell pepper
1 medium (12-ounce) jicama
  (see Note)

1. Cut the celery crosswise into 3-inch pieces, then lengthwise into ¼-inch strips. Cut the zucchini and cucumber the same way. Core and seed the peppers (the easiest way to do this is to cut the sides right off the core) and cut them into ¼-inch strips. Peel the jicama and cut it the same way.

2. Stand the vegetable sticks in bowls or arrange them on platters and serve with shallow bowls of the dips on pages 7 and 8.

Note: Jicama is a crisp root vegetable from Mexico that tastes like a cross between an apple and a potato.   *Serves 8 to 12*

20 CALORIES PER SERVING; 0.9 G PROTEIN; 0.1 G FAT; 0 G SATURATED FAT; 4 G CARBOHYDRATE; 15 MG SODIUM; 0 MG CHOLESTEROL

CAJUN DIP

3 tablespoons sweet paprika

2 tablespoons garlic powder

1 tablespoon freshly ground black pepper

1 tablespoon onion powder

1 tablespoon dried oregano

1 tablespoon dried thyme

1 teaspoon cayenne pepper

2 tablespoons kosher salt, or to taste

Put all the ingredients in a small bowl and whisk to combine.

Makes about ½ cup

7 CALORIES PER SERVING; 0.3 G PROTEIN: 0.2 G FAT; 0 G SATURATED FAT; 1.6 G CARBOHYDRATE; 534 MG SODIUM; 0 MG CHOLESTEROL

GREEK DIP

3 tablespoons dried oregano

1 tablespoon dried mint

1 tablespoon dried dill

1 tablespoon garlic flakes

2 teaspoons freshly ground black pepper

1 tablespoon kosher salt, or to taste

Put all the ingredients in a small bowl and whisk to combine.

Makes about ½ cup

4 CALORIES PER SERVING; 0.2 G PROTEIN; 0 G FAT; 0 G SATURATED FAT; 0.8 G CARBOHYDRATE; 267 MG SODIUM; 0 MG CHOLESTEROL

SHANGHAI DIP

2 tablespoons toasted white sesame seeds
2 tablespoons black sesame seeds
  (see page 52)
1 tablespoon poppy seeds

1 tablespoon onion flakes
1 tablespoon garlic flakes
2 teaspoons hot-pepper flakes

Put all the ingredients in a small bowl and whisk to combine.

Makes about ½ cup

23 CALORIES PER SERVING; 0.9 G PROTEIN; 1.8 G FAT; 0.2 G SATURATED FAT; 1.3 G CARBOHYDRATE; 5 MG SODIUM; 0 MG CHOLESTEROL

PROVENÇALE DIP

2 tablespoons dried basil
2 tablespoons dried oregano
1 tablespoon dried thyme
1 tablespoon dried marjoram

1 tablespoon dried rosemary
1 tablespoon dried lavender (optional)
1 tablespoon salt, or to taste

Put all the ingredients in a small bowl and whisk to combine.

Makes about ½ cup

7 CALORIES PER SERVING; 0.3 G PROTEIN; 0.2 G FAT; 0 G SATURATED FAT; 1.4 G CARBOHYDRATE; 1 MG SODIUM; 0 MG CHOLESTEROL

SKORDALIA (GREEK GARLIC-POTATO DIP)

Mashed potatoes flavored with dizzying doses of garlic and whipped to a creamy purée with lemon juice and olive oil—such is Greece's classical dip, Skordalia. *(*Skordo *is Greek for garlic.) Much of the oil in the traditional recipe has been replaced here with chicken or vegetable stock.*

2 medium baking potatoes (about 6 ounces each), peeled and quartered
6 to 8 cloves garlic, minced
Salt and freshly ground black pepper
2 tablespoons fresh lemon juice, or to taste

2 tablespoons extra-virgin olive oil
3 to 4 tablespoons chicken or vegetable stock
3 tablespoons chopped fresh parsley (preferably flat-leaf)

1. Put the potatoes in a saucepan, add cold water to cover and bring to a boil. Reduce the heat to a simmer and cook the potatoes until they are very soft, about 10 minutes. Drain well in a colander. Return the potatoes to the pot set over low heat for 2 minutes to dry them. Shake the pot so that the potatoes dry evenly and don't stick.

2. Put the garlic in a mixing bowl with a little salt and pepper. Mash the garlic to a paste with the back of a wooden spoon. Add the potatoes and mash them with a potato masher, or put them through a ricer. Using a wooden spoon, beat in the lemon juice, oil, and enough stock to obtain a light, creamy purée. Correct the seasoning with salt and lemon juice: the dip should be highly seasoned. Sprinkle with the parsley and serve with Pita Chips (see page 16) or your favorite crudités.

Note: For the best results, mash the potatoes by hand or with a ricer. Puréeing in the food processor will make the dip gummy.

Makes 2 cups, which will serve 8 to 10

71 CALORIES PER SERVING; 0.9 G PROTEIN; 3.4 G FAT; 0.5 G SATURATED FAT; 10 G CARBOHYDRATE; 3 MG SODIUM; 0 MG CHOLESTEROL

Spreads for Breads

Fig Tapenade

Tapenade—the olive, caper, and anchovy spread—is one of the classic hors d'oeuvres of Provence. Unfortunately for the health-conscious, its two main ingredients, olives and olive oil, are loaded with fat. I got an idea for a reduced-fat tapenade in Sarah Leah Chase's charming book The Bicycling Through Provence Cookbook, *which features a recipe for olive-and-fig tapenade. I've increased the proportion of figs to olives and replaced most of the olive oil with vegetable stock.*

2 cups dried black mission figs
   (about 10 ounces)
½ cup cognac
2 cups vegetable stock, chicken stock, or water
⅔ cup pitted oil- or brine-cured olives,
   such as kalamata
4 anchovy fillets, rinsed in warm water and

   patted dry
¼ cup drained capers
2 tablespoons Dijon-style mustard
2 tablespoons fresh lemon juice, or to taste
1 tablespoon extra-virgin olive oil
Salt and freshly ground black pepper
Toast points or slices of bread for serving

1. Stem and cut the figs crosswise into ¼-inch slices. Put them in a saucepan with the cognac and stock. Gently simmer 10 minutes, or until the figs are soft. Meanwhile, pit the olives.

2. Transfer the figs with a slotted spoon to a food processor, reserving the poaching liquid. Add the olives, anchovies, and capers, and process to a smooth paste. Add the mustard, lemon juice, and oil, and process to combine.

Fig Tapenade
Sun-Dried-Tomato Tartar
Roasted-Vegetable "Caviar"
Spicy Walnut Spread

With the motor running, add enough fig-poaching liquid (½ to 1 cup) to obtain a soft, spreadable purée. Correct the seasoning with salt, pepper, and lemon juice: the tapenade should be highly seasoned.

3. Transfer the tapenade to a serving bowl and serve with the toast points or bread.

Makes 2 cups, which will serve 8 to 10

162 CALORIES PER SERVING; 2 G PROTEIN; 6.6 G FAT; 0.9 G SATURATED FAT; 25 G CARBOHYDRATE; 588 MG SODIUM; 2 MG CHOLESTEROL

SUN-DRIED-TOMATO TARTAR

Remember the good old days when you could eat steak tartar without worrying about cholesterol or fat—or the even more serious risk of bacterial contamination from raw meat or eggs? Here's a "tartar" for the 1990s, made with sun-dried tomatoes instead of raw beef. When I have the time, I like to chop the tomatoes by hand with a cleaver rather than in the food processor. This gives them more the consistency of ground beef.

6 ounces dry-packed sun-dried tomatoes
(see Note)
5 anchovy fillets, rinsed, drained, and patted
dry (optional)
1 to 2 cloves garlic, minced
3 shallots, very finely chopped
(3 tablespoons)
1 to 2 tablespoons drained capers

2 tablespoons fresh lemon juice, or to taste
2 tablespoons extra-virgin olive oil
1 tablespoon Dijon-style mustard
1 tablespoon Worcestershire sauce
3 tablespoons chopped fresh parsley
(preferably flat-leaf), plus sprigs for garnish
Salt and freshly ground black pepper
Pumpernickel Toast Points (recipe follows)

1. Place the tomatoes in a small bowl and add hot water to cover. Let stand until the tomatoes are soft, about 15 minutes.

2. Drain the tomatoes, reserving the soaking liquid. Process the tomatoes in a food processor until coarsely chopped. Add the anchovy fillets, garlic, shallots, and capers, and process to combine. With the motor running, add the lemon juice, oil, mustard, Worcestershire sauce, and parsley. Season with a little salt and plenty of pepper. Add enough tomato-soaking liquid (3 to 4 tablespoons) to obtain a soft, spreadable

purée. Correct the seasoning with salt, pepper, lemon juice, or any of the other flavorings: the tartar should be highly seasoned.

3. Mound the mixture on a serving plate or in a bowl. Garnish it with the parsley sprigs and serve with Pumpernickel Toast Points.

Note: The results will be even better if you make your own sun-dried tomatoes from scratch, following the recipe in my book *High-Flavor, Low-Fat Vegetarian Cooking.*

Makes 3 cups, which will serve 10 to 12

85 CALORIES PER SERVING; 3.3 G PROTEIN; 3.3 G FAT; 0.6 G SATURATED FAT; 13 G CARBOHYDRATE; 212 MG SODIUM; 3 MG CHOLESTEROL

PUMPERNICKEL TOAST POINTS

½ package thinly sliced cocktail-type mini-loaves of pumpernickel bread (22 slices)

1 tablespoon extra-virgin olive oil or spray oil

1. Preheat the oven to 375° F. Cut each pumpernickel slice on the diagonal and lightly brush each slice with oil on both sides or spray with spray oil.

2. Arrange the slices on a baking sheet and bake until crisp, 10 to 15 minutes per side. Transfer the toast points to a cooling rack.

Makes 44 toast points

95 CALORIES PER SERVING; 3 G PROTEIN; 1.8 G FAT; 0.3 G SATURATED FAT; 18 G CARBOHYDRATE; 193 MG SODIUM; 0 MG CHOLESTEROL

Roasted-Vegetable "Caviar"

Vegetable "caviars" are a popular Russian appetizer, not to mention the specialty of my friend the late Bob Ginn. While this one won't fool anyone into thinking he's eating beluga, it does have the soft, crunchy-gooey texture one associates with caviar and a robust flavor that would do any zakuski platter (Russian hors d'oeuvres) proud. My low-fat version calls for the vegetables to be roasted in a super-hot oven—a technique that provides so much flavor, you only need a fraction of the oil found in the traditional recipe.

1 medium eggplant (10 to 12 ounces)
1 medium onion, peeled and quartered
½ green bell pepper, cored and seeded
½ red bell pepper, cored and seeded
1 carrot, peeled and cut into chunks
1 large ripe tomato, halved and seeded
  (see page xiv)
1 large or 2 small stalks celery, thinly sliced
2 jalapeño chilies or other hot peppers, halved
  and seeded (optional)
3 cloves garlic, peeled
Spray oil

TO FINISH THE "CAVIAR":
¼ cup chopped fresh parsley
  (preferably flat-leaf)
3 tablespoons chopped fresh dill or cilantro
1 to 2 tablespoons fresh lemon juice,
  or to taste
1 to 2 tablespoons extra-virgin olive oil
Salt and freshly ground black pepper

1. Preheat the oven to 450° F. Lightly spray a nonstick baking sheet with spray oil. Prick the eggplant in several places with a fork. Place the eggplant, onion, bell peppers, carrot, tomato, celery, jalapeños, and 2 cloves of the garlic on the prepared baking sheet. (Place the garlic, celery, and jalapeños on top of the tomatoes to keep them from burning.) Roast the vegetables until very tender, 20 to 30 minutes. Stir as needed to prevent scorching. Remove the pan from the oven and let the vegetables cool to room temperature.

2. Transfer the onion, carrot, tomato, celery, garlic, and jalapeños to a food processor and process in bursts until coarsely chopped. Cut the eggplant in half lengthwise, scrape out the pulp with a spoon, and add it to the processor along with the bell peppers. Process in bursts

until coarsely chopped. Mince the remaining 1 clove garlic and add along with the parsley, dill, lemon juice, and oil. Season with salt and pepper, and process to mix. Correct the seasoning with salt and lemon juice: the "caviar" should be highly seasoned. Chill and serve with Pita Chips (see below) or Pumpernickel Toast Points (see page 14).

Note: Alternatively, you could spoon the "caviar" into hollowed-out mushroom caps or zucchini halves and bake in a 400° F. oven until thoroughly heated, 10 to 15 minutes.

Makes about 2½ cups, which will serve 8 to 10

43 CALORIES PER SERVING; 9 G PROTEIN; 1.9 G FAT; 3 G SATURATED FAT; 6.6 G CARBOHYDRATE; 12 MG SODIUM; 0 MG CHOLESTEROL

PITA CHIPS

Pita chips are great for dipping—not to mention for using up leftover pita bread.

3 large or 4 small pita breads
1 tablespoon extra-virgin olive oil (optional)

1 tablespoon sesame seeds

1. Preheat the oven to 350° F. Separate the pita breads and brush the rough side of the pita with the olive oil, if using. Cut each piece into 8 wedges (6 wedges for small breads) and sprinkle with sesame seeds.

2. Arrange the wedges on a baking sheet and bake 8 to 10 minutes, or until golden brown. Transfer the wedges to a cooling rack.

Makes 48 wedges

7 CALORIES PER SERVING; 0.2 G PROTEIN; 0 G FAT; 1 G CARBOHYDRATE; 13 MG SODIUM; 0 MG CHOLESTEROL

SPICY WALNUT SPREAD

Walnuts might seem an unlikely ingredient for a low-fat dip, since nuts are quite high in fat. But by toasting the nuts you intensify their flavor, so a relatively small quantity goes a long way.

32 ounces nonfat plain yogurt
½ cup shelled walnuts
1 teaspoon ground coriander
½ teaspoon ground cumin

½ teaspoon hot-pepper flakes
Salt and freshly ground black pepper
2 tablespoons chopped fresh cilantro or
   parsley (preferably flat-leaf)

1. Drain the yogurt overnight in a yogurt strainer or a regular strainer lined with a cheesecloth or paper towels.

2. Preheat the oven to 400° F. Arrange the walnuts on a baking sheet in a single layer and bake until fragrant and lightly toasted, about 5 minutes. Transfer the walnuts to a plate and let cool. Set aside 2 or 3 walnut halves for garnish.

3. Put the walnuts in a food processor and process in bursts until finely ground. Add the drained yogurt, coriander, cumin, and hot-pepper flakes and process to combine. Season with salt and pepper: the spread should be highly seasoned. Stir in the cilantro by hand.

4. Transfer the spread to a serving bowl and serve with Bruschette (see page 58), Pita Chips (see page 16), or Pumpernickel Toast Points (see page 14).

Makes 1¾ cups, which will serve 6 to 8

111 CALORIES PER SERVING; 8 G PROTEIN; 6 G FAT; 0.4 G SATURATED FAT; 6 G CARBOHYDRATE; 49 MG SODIUM; 0 MG CHOLESTEROL

WRAPS AND ROLLS

SANTA FE "SUSHI"

You won't find this dish at any sushi bar, but the colorful assortment of tuna, avocado, tomato, and scallion rolled in a tortilla recalls some of Japan's maki (seaweed, rice, and fish rolls). You could also use cooked shrimp (see Note).

12 ounces fresh tuna steak
2 teaspoons extra-virgin olive oil
2 teaspoons chili powder
Salt and freshly ground black pepper
2 poblano chilies or 1 green bell pepper
1 yellow bell pepper (optional)
8 ounces fresh spinach, stemmed

FOR THE CHILI CREAM SAUCE:
1 cup nonfat sour cream
1 tablespoon fresh lime juice
2 teaspoons chili powder

½ teaspoon ground cumin
Salt and freshly ground black pepper

TO FINISH THE "SUSHI":
4 8-inch flour tortillas
1 ripe avocado
1 tomato, peeled and seeded (see page xiv)
1 bunch cilantro, separated into sprigs
8 pickled jalapeño chilies, thinly sliced
   lengthwise (optional)
8 scallions, green part only

1. Brush the tuna with the oil on both sides, sprinkle with the chili powder, and season with salt and pepper. Heat a nonstick frying pan over high heat. Sear the tuna on both sides (1 to 2 minutes per side for rare, 2 to 3 minutes per side for medium). Transfer the tuna to a plate and let cool. (Alternatively, the tuna can be grilled or broiled.)

2. Roast and peel the poblano and yellow pepper (see page 60). Cut them into long, ¼-inch strips. Blanch the spinach in boiling salted water until tender, about 30 seconds.

Drain, chill in ice water, drain again, and blot dry with paper towels.

2. Make the chili cream sauce: Put the sour cream, lime juice, chili powder, and cumin in a nonreactive mixing bowl and whisk to combine. Season with salt and pepper: the sauce should be highly seasoned. Place half the cream sauce in a small serving bowl to serve as a dipping sauce.

3. Preheat the oven to 350° F. Place the tortillas on a baking sheet and heat until soft and pliable, 2 to 3 minutes. Meanwhile, peel and pit the avocado and cut it into long, ¼-inch strips. Cut the tomato into long, ¼-inch strips. Slice the tuna into long, ¼-inch strips.

4. To assemble the "sushi," lay a tortilla on a work surface. Spread 1 tablespoon of the remaining cream sauce evenly over the surface. Arrange a thin layer of spinach on top of this. Starting at the edge closest to you, arrange strips of tuna, avocado, tomato, roasted peppers, cilantro, jalapeño, and scallion in neat horizontal rows, leaving the last inch of tortilla uncovered. Roll up the tortilla tightly and wrap in plastic wrap. Repeat with the remaining tortillas. Let the "sushi" stand 10 minutes before cutting.

5. Just before serving, using a very sharp, slender knife, cut each "sushi" roll crosswise into 1-inch sections. (Do not serve end sections that look ragged.) Stand the sections on end and arrange them on a platter around the bowl of dipping sauce.

Note: You can substitute 16 large, peeled, and deveined shrimp for the tuna. Impale them end to end on a bamboo skewer to keep them straight during cooking. Poach in simmering water until just firm, about 1 minute. Season with salt and pepper, omitting the chili powder.

Makes 4 to 5 dozen pieces

33 CALORIES PER PIECE; 2.5 G PROTEIN; 1.3 G FAT; 0.3 G SATURATED FAT; 3 G CARBOHYDRATE; 27 MG SODIUM; 3 MG CHOLESTEROL

CRAB QUESADILLA

Ten years ago, few North Americans had even heard of quesadillas. Today, you can hardly dine anywhere without encountering these Mexican grilled-cheese "sandwiches" made with flour tortillas instead of bread. Here's a version inspired by the place where I grew up, Baltimore, where crab is king.

½ pound crabmeat (see Note)
⅔ cup nonfat sour cream
2 teaspoons Old Bay Seasoning, or to taste
   (see Note)
½ cup grated sharp cheddar cheese
   (about 2 ounces) (optional)
4 scallions, trimmed and finely chopped

1 tomato, seeded and finely diced (see page xiv)
½ cup cooked corn kernels (fresh, frozen,
   or canned)
3 to 4 tablespoons fresh cilantro leaves
1 to 2 pickled jalapeño chilies, thinly sliced
   (optional)
8 8-inch flour tortillas

1. Preheat the grill or broiler to medium-high. Pick through the crabmeat to remove any bits of shell. Put the sour cream in a mixing bowl and stir in the crabmeat, Old Bay Seasoning, cheese, scallion, tomato, corn, cilantro, and jalapeños. Correct the seasoning with Old Bay Seasoning.

2. Lay 4 of the tortillas on a work surface. Spread the crab mixture evenly over them, using a spatula or the back of a spoon. Place the remaining tortillas on top to make a sandwich.

3. Grill or broil the quesadillas until the tortillas are lightly browned and the filling is heated through. (Alternatively, you can cook the quesadillas in a dry nonstick frying pan set over high heat until the tortillas brown and blister, 1 to 2 minutes per side.) Cut each quesadilla into 8 wedges and serve at once.

Note: There are several options for the crabmeat: backfin lump meat from the blue crab (my favorite), delicate shreds of Maine crab, Dungeness crab, or even king crab. You could also make these quesadillas with cooked or smoked shrimp. Old Bay Seasoning is a spice blend manufactured in Baltimore and traditionally used for steaming crabs. It's available in most supermarkets and gourmet shops.   *Makes 48 wedges*

24 CALORIES PER PIECE; 1.5 G PROTEIN; 0.4 G FAT; 0.1 G SATURATED FAT; 3.6 G CARBOHYDRATE; 43 MG SODIUM; 4 MG CHOLESTEROL

SCALLION BLINTZES

This recipe was inspired by a dish I never actually tasted: zibulnikas—scallion cheese buns. My grandfather spoke so lovingly of these Judeo-Latvian pastries (a specialty of his mother, Grandma Raichlen), I can almost taste them. The cheese mixture (or, at least, how I imagine it) makes a great filling for crepes. If you feel like a splurge, brush the blintzes with melted butter before baking.

FOR THE FILLING:
32 ounces no- or low-fat cottage cheese
2 large egg whites or 1 large egg, lightly
    beaten
1 bunch scallions, trimmed and finely
    chopped
1 teaspoon grated lemon zest

1 teaspoon fresh lemon juice, or to taste
Salt and freshly ground black pepper

Spray oil
16 Buttermilk Crepes (recipe follows)
No- or low-fat sour cream for garnish

1. Place a large strainer over a bowl, add the cottage cheese, and let drain in the refrigerator for at least 3 hours or overnight. Make the crepes while the cheese is draining.

2. Make the filling: Put the cottage cheese, egg whites, scallion, zest, and lemon juice in a nonreactive mixing bowl, season with salt and pepper, and stir to combine.

3. Lightly spray a large baking dish with spray oil. Place a crepe on the work surface, pale side up. Place 2 to 3 tablespoons of the filling in the center. Roll up the crepe tightly, folding in the side flaps halfway through. Transfer the blintzes to the prepared baking dish. (The blintzes can be made several hours ahead to this stage and refrigerated.)

4. Preheat the oven to 400° F. Spray the tops of the blintzes with oil. Bake the blintzes until the filling is thoroughly heated and set and the tops are golden brown, 10 to 15 minutes. Serve at once with dollops of sour cream on the side.

Makes 14 to 16 small blintzes

83 CALORIES PER PIECE; 8 G PROTEIN; 0.9 G FAT; 1.1 G SATURATED FAT; 8 G CARBOHYDRATE; 172 MG SODIUM; 19 MG CHOLESTEROL

BUTTERMILK CREPES

Every nation has its version of pancakes, from Russian blini to Jewish blintzes. The most famous of all is France's gossamer crepe. My low-fat version reduces the number of egg yolks and uses buttermilk to achieve the richness once acquired with butter and cream.

1 large egg plus 2 egg whites, beaten
½ cup low-fat buttermilk
¾ cup water
½ teaspoon sugar

½ teaspoon salt, or to taste
1 teaspoon canola oil
1 cup unbleached white flour
Spray oil

1. Put the egg, egg whites, buttermilk, water, sugar, salt, and oil in a mixing bowl and whisk to combine. Sift in the flour and gently whisk just to combine. (Do not overmix, or the crepes will be rubbery.) If the batter is lumpy, strain it. The batter should be the consistency of heavy cream; if it is too thick, thin it with a little more water.

2. Lightly spray a crepe pan or 7-inch frying pan with oil and heat over medium heat. (When the pan is the proper temperature, a drop of water falling on it will evaporate in 2 to 3 seconds.) Off the heat, add a shot glass full or 1 small ladleful of batter (about 3 tablespoons) to the pan. Gently tilt and rotate the pan to coat the bottom with a thin layer of batter. (Pour back any excess: the crepe should be as thin as possible.)

3. Cook the crepe until it is lightly browned on both sides, 30 to 60 seconds per side, turning it with a spatula. As the crepes are done, stack them on a plate. For the best results, spray the pan with oil after every crepe.

Note: For extra flavor, replace ¼ cup of the flour with buckwheat flour or stone-ground fine cornmeal, use cider or beer in place of the water, or add 2 tablespoons minced chives.

Makes 16 crepes

42 CALORIES PER CREPE; 2 G PROTEIN; 1 G FAT; 0.2 G SATURATED FAT; 0.6 G CARBOHYDRATE; 78 MG SODIUM; 13 MG CHOLESTEROL

CAMBODIAN SALAD ROLLS (*Nym Chao*)

Rhode Island is, of course, famous for its seafood (see the recipe for Stuffies on page 39). What you may not know is that Providence is home to a large Cambodian community and an excellent place to try nym chao (nym rhymes with "dime"), Cambodian salad rolls. Nym chao are like Vietnamese spring rolls: a refreshing blend of noodles and herbs rolled in rice paper. The following recipe comes from my friend New England food broadcast journalist Barry Nelson, who learned to make nym chao from his Cambodian neighbor.

4 ounces rice vermicelli or bean threads (see Note)
3 cups mung bean sprouts (about 8 ounces)
1 head Boston lettuce, separated into leaves
16 9-inch or 24 6-inch round rice papers (see Note)
1 carrot, peeled and finely shredded
1 bunch fresh cilantro, stemmed
1 bunch fresh mint, stemmed
1 bunch garlic chives (Chinese chives) or 1 to 2 bunches scallions, green part only, white part reserved for the dipping sauce
1 bunch basil (preferably Thai), stemmed (see Note)

FOR THE DIPPING SAUCE:
½ cup soy sauce
½ cup fish sauce (see Note)
½ cup distilled vinegar, or to taste
¼ cup sugar, or to taste
3 cloves garlic, minced
3 scallions, white part only, finely chopped
1 to 3 teaspoons chili paste or hot sauce
¼ cup finely chopped dry-roasted peanuts (either salted or unsalted, according to taste)

1. Soak the noodles in cold water until soft, about 20 minutes. Drain well and cut four or five times with scissors.

2. Place the bean sprouts in a colander and pour boiling water over them. Flatten the lettuce leaves with the side of a cleaver or cut the stems out, so that each leaf is pliable. Tear any large leaves into pieces half the size of the rice paper.

3. Fill a large, shallow bowl with cold water. Soak a sheet of rice paper in the water 1 minute. Carefully transfer the rice paper to a clean

dish towel placed on a cutting board and let sit 1 to 2 minutes, or until soft and pliable. Blot dry with paper towels.

4. Assemble the salad rolls: Place a piece of lettuce on top of the rice paper. Place a small mound of bean sprouts, shredded carrot, noodles, cilantro, mint, and garlic chives on top. Begin tightly rolling up the rice paper. After the first turn, arrange a row of basil leaves on the rice paper running parallel to the roll, and continue rolling, folding in the side flaps halfway up. The idea is to form a compact roll about 5 inches long, with the basil showing through the rice paper. Assemble the remaining salad rolls the same way. (The assembled rolls will keep for up to 24 hours covered with plastic wrap in the refrigerator.)

5. Make the dipping sauce: Put the soy sauce, fish sauce, vinegar, sugar, garlic, scallion, chili paste, and peanuts in a nonreactive mixing bowl and whisk to combine and dissolve the sugar. Correct the seasoning with fish sauce, sugar, or vinegar: the sauce should be a little sweet, a little sour, and a little salty.

Serve the salad rolls with the dipping sauce.

Note: Rice vermicelli are hair-thin rice noodles; bean threads are thin noodles made from mung bean starch and sold in small net packages. Rice paper is a type of noodle made from rice flour. It comes in fragile, paper-thin sheets that shatter like glass if mishandled. But soak rice papers in cold water and they become as soft and pliable as crepes. Thai basil has smaller leaves and a more licoricy flavor than regular basil. Fish sauce is a Southeast Asian condiment made from pickled anchovies. These ingredients can be found in Asian markets, natural foods stores, gourmet shops, and many supermarkets.

Makes 16 large or 24 small rolls

78 CALORIES PER ROLL; 3.5 G PROTEIN; 1.2 G FAT; 0.3 G SATURATED FAT; 14 G CARBOHYDRATE; 1,216 MG SODIUM; 0 MG CHOLESTEROL

DUMPLINGS AND PASTRIES

EMPANADAS (HISPANIC MEAT PIES)

Empanadas are a popular snack from one end of Latin America to the other. The juxtaposition of sweet and salty flavors (raisins, capers, and olives) is a hallmark of Hispanic cooking. Traditionally, empanadas are filled with pork, made with a lard-based dough, and deep-fried. This recipe (made with chicken) achieves a similar crispness with a lot less fat—and a lot less work—by using ravioli wrappers (available in the produce section of most supermarkets) and baking the empanadas in the oven.

FOR THE FILLING:
8 ounces boneless, skinless chicken breast
1 clove garlic, finely chopped
½ small onion, finely chopped (about ¼ cup)
½ green bell pepper, cored, seeded, and finely chopped
½ tomato, seeded and coarsely chopped (see page xiv)
1 tablespoon tomato paste
2 tablespoons chicken stock or water
½ teaspoon cumin, or to taste

2 tablespoons raisins
4 pimiento-stuffed green olives, coarsely chopped
1 teaspoon minced fresh cilantro or parsley (preferably flat-leaf)
Salt and freshly ground black pepper
1 to 2 tablespoons dry bread crumbs

TO FINISH THE EMPANADAS:
36 3-inch round ravioli wrappers
Spray oil or olive oil

1. Prepare the filling: Wash and dry the chicken breast and trim off any fat or sinew. Cut the chicken into ½-inch dice. Put the chicken, garlic, onion, green pepper, tomato, tomato paste, stock, cumin, raisins, olives, and cilantro in a saucepan, and season with salt and pepper.

Gently simmer over medium heat, stirring often, until the chicken is cooked, about 5 minutes.

2. Transfer the mixture to a food processor and process until coarsely ground. The mixture should be fairly dry; if it is too wet, add 1 to 2 tablespoons bread crumbs. Correct the seasoning with cumin or salt: the filling should be highly seasoned. Refrigerate until cold.

3. Preheat the oven to 400° F. Lightly spray or brush a baking sheet (preferably nonstick) with oil. Arrange a few ravioli wrappers on a work surface. Very lightly brush the edge of each wrapper with water (this acts as glue to make a seal). Place a heaping teaspoon of the filling in the center and fold the wrapper in half to make a half-moon-shaped dumpling. Crimp the edges with a fork. Place the empanadas on a wire rack and repeat the process with the rest of the ravioli wrappers.

4. Arrange the empanadas on the prepared baking sheet. Spray or brush the tops of the empanadas with oil. Bake the empanadas until the pastry is crisp and golden brown on both sides, 4 to 6 minutes per side.   *Makes 36 empanadas*

22 CALORIES PER PIECE; 1.5 G PROTEIN; 0.4 G FAT; 0 G SATURATED FAT; 3 G CARBOHYDRATE; 16 MG SODIUM; 6 MG CHOLESTEROL

SAMOSAS (INDIAN SPICED POTATO TURNOVERS)

Samosas are one of India's national snacks—crisp, flaky turnovers often filled with spicy, but not fiery, potatoes. The traditional version is deep-fried, but delicious samosas can be made using wonton wrappers and baking instead of frying. You could also wrap the filling in filo dough.

FOR THE FILLING:
1 large or 2 small baking potatoes
  (about 10 ounces)
1 small onion, grated (about ½ cup)
½ cup cooked green peas
1 tablespoon minced fresh ginger
1 to 2 jalapeño chilies, seeded and minced
  (for a hotter samosa, leave in the seeds)
½ teaspoon garam masala (optional)
  (see Note)
½ teaspoon ground coriander (1 teaspoon if
  not using garam masala)

¼ teaspoon cumin seeds, toasted (see Note)
¼ teaspoon ground cardamom
3 tablespoons minced fresh cilantro
1 tablespoon fresh lemon juice, or to taste
2 tablespoons sesame seeds, toasted
  (see Note)
Salt and freshly ground black pepper

TO FINISH THE SAMOSAS:
36 4-inch square wonton wrappers
Spray oil or olive oil

1. Cook the potatoes, unpeeled, in 3 quarts boiling salted water until very tender, 15 to 20 minutes. Drain in a colander and rinse with cold water until the potatoes are cool enough to handle. Peel the potatoes and coarsely grate them.

2. Put the potatoes, onion, peas, ginger, jalapeños, garam masala, ground coriander, cumin, cardamom, cilantro, lemon juice, and 1 tablespoon of the sesame seeds in a nonreactive mixing bowl, season with salt and pepper, and

stir to combine. Correct the seasoning with salt, spices, or lemon juice: the filling should be highly seasoned. Let the mixture cool to room temperature.

3. Preheat the oven to 400° F. Arrange a few wonton wrappers on a work surface. Very lightly brush the edges of each wrapper with water (this acts as glue to make a seal). Place a heaping spoonful of the filling in the center and fold the wrapper in half on the diagonal. Press the edges with your fingertips to seal. Place the

samosas on a wire rack and repeat the process with the rest of the wonton wrappers.

4. Lightly spray or brush a baking sheet (preferably nonstick) with oil and arrange the samosas on the prepared baking sheet. Spray or brush the tops of the samosas with oil and sprinkle with the remaining sesame seeds. Bake the samosas until the pastry is crisp and golden brown on both sides, 4 to 6 minutes per side.

Note: *Garam masala* is an Indian spice mix that includes coriander, cardamom, black pepper, bay leaves, nutmeg, and cloves. A simple recipe for garam masala can be found in my books *High-Flavor, Low-Fat Cooking* and *High-Flavor, Low-Fat Vegetarian Cooking*. Toasting the cumin and sesame seeds is optional, but it does intensify their flavor. Place them in a dry skillet over medium heat. Cook until fragrant and just beginning to brown, about 5 minutes, shaking the pan to ensure even toasting. Transfer the seeds to a bowl to cool.

Makes 36 samosas

22 CALORIES PER PIECE; 0.7 G PROTEIN; 0.4 G FAT; 0 G SATURATED FAT; 4 G CARBOHYDRATE; 3 MG SODIUM; 2 MG CHOLESTEROL

SEAFOOD POT STICKERS
WITH HONEY-SOY DIPPING SAUCE

Pot stickers are pan-fried Chinese pork dumplings. I've lightened the traditional recipe by using seafood instead of pork.
This recipe calls for equal amounts of shrimp and scallops, but you can use only shrimp if you prefer.

FOR THE FILLING:
8-ounce can water chestnuts, drained
4 ounces peeled and deveined shrimp
   (5 ounces if buying shrimp with shells on)
4 ounces scallops
1 clove garlic, minced
2 scallions, trimmed and minced
1 tablespoon minced fresh ginger
2 teaspoons soy sauce

1 teaspoon sugar
Salt and freshly ground black pepper

TO FINISH THE POT STICKERS:
36 3-inch round ravioli wrappers
Canola oil
½ cup water

Honey-Soy Dipping Sauce (see page 33)

1. Finely chop the water chestnuts by hand or in a food processor and transfer to a mixing bowl. Coarsely chop the shrimp and scallops in the food processor. Add the garlic, scallion, ginger, soy sauce, and sugar, season with salt and pepper, and pulse to mix. Stir the seafood mixture into the water chestnuts. Correct the seasoning with salt: the filling should be highly seasoned. (To taste for seasoning without eating raw seafood, cook a tiny bit on the end of a spoon in boiling water.)

2. Arrange a few ravioli wrappers on a work surface. Very lightly brush the edges of each wrapper with water (this acts as glue to make a

seal). Place a teaspoon of the filling in the center and fold the wrapper in half to make a half-moon-shaped dumpling. Press the edges with your fingertips or crimp with a fork to seal. Place the pot stickers on a wire rack and repeat the process with the rest of the ravioli wrappers.

3. Heat 1 to 2 teaspoons oil in a large non-stick frying pan or sauté pan. Set over high heat. Arrange a single layer of pot stickers in the pan and cook, shaking the pan to prevent them from sticking, until the bottoms are nicely browned, 1 to 2 minutes. Turn the dumplings, add the water to the pan, and bring to a boil.

Cover and cook 2 minutes. Remove the cover and continue cooking until all the water has evaporated and the bottoms of the dumplings are browned, 2 to 3 minutes. Transfer the dumplings to a platter and keep warm in a 200° F. oven or on a warming shelf over the stove.

Cook the remaining dumplings in this fashion, adding more oil as necessary.

4. Arrange the pot stickers on a serving platter and serve with Honey-Soy Dipping Sauce.

Makes 36 dumplings

22 CALORIES PER PIECE; 2 G PROTEIN; 0.6 G FAT; 0.1 G SATURATED FAT; 3 G CARBOHYDRATE; 30 MG SODIUM; 9 MG CHOLESTEROL

HONEY-SOY DIPPING SAUCE

Here's a sweet-and-sour sauce for people who don't like sweet-and-sour sauce.
There's nothing sticky or cloying about it.

⅔ cup low-sodium soy sauce
⅔ cup distilled vinegar
¼ cup honey, or to taste
¼ cup water, or to taste

3 cloves garlic, minced
1 tablespoon minced fresh ginger
3 scallions, trimmed and minced

Put all the ingredients in a nonreactive mixing bowl and whisk to combine. If the sauce tastes too strong, add a little more water; if it's too salty, add a little more honey. Transfer the sauce to small bowls for dipping.

Makes 1¾ cups

11 CALORIES PER SERVING (2 TEASPOONS); 0.3 G PROTEIN; 0 G FAT; 0 G SATURATED FAT;
2.7 G CARBOHYDRATE; 179 MG SODIUM; 0 MG CHOLESTEROL

OVEN-BAKED EGGROLLS

My discovery that eggroll and wonton wrappers could be baked instead of deep-fried came as a revelation. (Like many revelations, it was an accident—a last-ditch attempt to salvage some soggy steamed dumplings.) To keep my family happy, I've made these eggrolls vegetarian, but you could always add a little chopped cooked pork or shrimp.

FOR THE FILLING:
5 dried Chinese black mushrooms
8 ounces nappa (Chinese cabbage) or savoy
    cabbage, julienned (about 2 cups; ¼ to
    ½ cabbage, depending on size)
2 carrots, julienned (about 1 cup)
8-ounce can water chestnuts, julienned
4 ounces snapped and strung snow peas,
    julienned (about 1 cup)
2 stalks celery, julienned (about ¼ cup)
5 ounces mung bean sprouts (about 2 cups)

FOR THE COOKING SAUCE:
1 tablespoon cornstarch
1 tablespoon soy sauce

1 tablespoon rice wine or dry sherry
1 tablespoon oyster sauce
1 tablespoon sugar or honey
Freshly ground black pepper

1 tablespoon canola oil
3 cloves garlic, minced
3 scallions, trimmed and minced
1 tablespoon slivered fresh ginger

36 to 40 4-inch square wonton wrappers
2 teaspoons cornstarch dissolved in
    2 teaspoons cold water to make paste
Spray oil or canola oil

1. Soak the mushrooms in hot water for 30 minutes. Drain and squeeze the mushrooms, reserving the soaking liquid for soups and sauces if desired. Stem the mushrooms and julienne. Put the mushrooms, cabbage, carrots, water chestnuts, snow peas, celery, and bean sprouts in a mixing bowl and stir to combine.

2. Put the cornstarch, soy sauce, wine, oyster sauce, and sugar in a small bowl, season with pepper, and whisk to combine.

3. Heat a wok (preferably nonstick) over high heat to smoking. Swirl in the canola oil. Add the garlic, scallion, and ginger, and stir-fry 30 seconds, or until fragrant but not browned. Add the vegetable mixture and stir-fry until the vegetables are crisp-tender and most of the liq-

uid has evaporated, 4 to 5 minutes. Stir the sauce and add it to the wok. Bring the mixture to a boil: the sauce will thicken. Transfer the mixture to a bowl and let cool to room temperature, then refrigerate until cold. (If you're in a hurry, chill the bowl over ice.) The filling can be prepared ahead to this stage.

4. Preheat the oven to 450° F. Lightly spray or brush a nonstick baking sheet with oil. Arrange a wonton wrapper on a work surface on the diagonal, with a point facing you. Place about 1 tablespoonful of filling in the center.

Fold the bottom third (the side closest to you) over the filling, then fold in the sides. Roll up the eggroll, securing the end with a dab of cornstarch paste. Assemble the remaining eggrolls the same way, placing the finished ones on the prepared baking sheet.

5. Lightly spray or brush the tops of the eggrolls with oil. Bake until crisp and golden brown on both sides, 15 to 20 minutes. Serve at once with Chinese mustard and duck sauce or Honey-Soy Dipping Sauce (see page 33).

Makes 36 to 40 2-inch eggrolls

44 CALORIES PER PIECE; 1.4 G PROTEIN; 1.2 G FAT; 0.1 G SATURATED FAT; 7 G CARBOHYDRATE; 67 MG SODIUM; 2 MG CHOLESTEROL

IN A SHELL

SALSA-STEAMED MUSSELS

This recipe is simplicity itself, but it never fails to fetch raves. Half the salsa is used for steaming the mussels; the other half serves as a topping.

FOR THE SALSA:

2 to 3 ripe tomatoes, seeded and finely chopped (about 2 cups) (see page xiv)

1 to 3 serrano or jalapeño chilies, seeded and chopped (for a hotter salsa, leave in the seeds)

½ medium red onion, finely chopped (about ½ cup)

2 cloves garlic, minced

½ cup chopped fresh cilantro

¼ cup fresh lime juice, or to taste

Salt and freshly ground black pepper

2 pounds mussels (about 45 medium mussels)

2 cups dry white wine

FOR THE GARNISH:

¼ cup nonfat sour cream

45 small cilantro sprigs (optional)

1. Prepare the salsa: Put the tomatoes, chilies, onion, garlic, cilantro, and lime juice in a nonreactive mixing bowl, season with salt and pepper, and mix to combine. Correct the seasoning with salt or lime juice: the salsa should be highly seasoned.

2. Scrub the mussels with a stiff brush under cold running water, discarding any with cracked shells or shells that fail to close when tapped. Remove the cluster of threads at the hinge of the mussels by pinching the threads between your thumb and the back of a paring knife and pulling, or using needlenose pliers.

3. Put half the salsa in a large, heavy pot

with a tight-fitting lid. Add the wine and bring to a boil. Add the mussels, cover, and cook until the mussels open wide, 5 to 8 minutes. Stir the mussels once or twice during the cooking so that the shells on the bottom have room to open. Transfer the mussels with a slotted spoon to a colander set over a bowl and let cool. (The leftover broth makes a great base for soups.)

4. Remove the top shell from each mussel and discard. Arrange the bottom shells on a platter. Top each mussel with a spoonful of salsa. Whisk the sour cream until smooth, then transfer it to a squirt bottle. Squirt a squiggle of sour cream on each mussel. (Or place a tiny dollop of sour cream on each mussel with a spoon.) Garnish with cilantro sprigs. The mussels can be prepared several hours ahead and refrigerated. Serve at room temperature.

Serves 6 to 8

84 CALORIES PER SERVING; 16 G PROTEIN; 1 G FAT; 0.2 G SATURATED FAT; 6 G CARBOHYDRATE; 156 MG SODIUM; 13 MG CHOLESTEROL

STUFFIES (RHODE ISLAND STUFFED CLAMS)

I like to think of the following as low-fat clams casino. The recipe is based on Rhode Island's official state snack, stuffies (stuffed clams). A Rhode Islander would use a quahog (the large hardshell clam favored by New Englanders for making chowder). Littleneck or cherrystone make for better finger fare, but any size clam will do.

36 littleneck clams, 24 cherrystone clams,
   or 12 quahogs
2 cups cool water
1½ teaspoons extra-virgin olive oil
1 small onion, finely chopped
2 shallots, finely chopped
2 stalks celery, finely chopped
2 cloves garlic, minced
1 scallion, finely chopped
1 tablespoon fresh or 1 teaspoon dried
   marjoram
1 teaspoon fresh or dried thyme

1 tablespoon fresh or 1 teaspoon dried
   oregano
2 teaspoons grated lemon zest
5 tablespoons finely chopped parsley
   (preferably flat-leaf)
2 cups fresh bread crumbs, lightly toasted,
   plus more as needed
1 to 2 tablespoons fresh lemon juice
1 teaspoon hot sauce (optional)
Salt and freshly ground black pepper
Cayenne pepper

1. Scrub the clams with a stiff brush under cold running water to remove any sand. Place the clams in a large pot with a tight-fitting lid. Add the water, cover, bring to a boil, and cook until the shells just begin to open, about 5 minutes for cherrystones or littlenecks, 10 to 15 minutes for quahogs. Transfer the clams with a slotted spoon to a plate to cool. Strain the cooking liquid through a cheesecloth or paper-towel-lined sieve and reserve 1½ cups. (Any excess can be saved for chowders or stews.)

2. Remove the meat from the clamshells, reserving the bottoms of the shells. Finely chop the clam meat in a food processor or meat grinder or by hand, reserving the juices.

3. Heat the oil in a large nonstick frying pan. Add the onion, shallot, celery, and garlic, and cook over medium heat until the vegetables just begin to brown, about 5 minutes. Add the chopped clams, scallion, marjoram, thyme,

oregano, and zest, and 4 tablespoons of the parsley, and cook 1 minute. Remove the pan from the heat.

4. Put the bread crumbs, lemon juice, and hot sauce and 1 cup of the reserved clam broth in a nonreactive mixing bowl. Stir in the clam mixture and season with salt, pepper, and cayenne. If the mixture is too dry, add a little more clam broth; if it's too wet, add a few more bread crumbs. Spoon the clam mixture into the reserved shells, mounding it high in the center. The stuffies can be prepared ahead to this stage and refrigerated; they can even be frozen.

5. Arrange the broiler rack 6 inches under the heating element and preheat the broiler. Broil the stuffies until thoroughly heated and golden brown on top, about 15 minutes. Sprinkle with the remaining 1 tablespoon parsley and serve at once.   *Serves 6 to 8*

49 CALORIES PER SERVING; 6 G PROTEIN; 0.9 G FAT; 0.1 G SATURATED FAT; 4 G CARBOHYDRATE; 48 MG SODIUM; 15 MG CHOLESTEROL

GOLDEN BASKETS

This classic Thai appetizer features crisp pastry cups filled with spiced ground chicken or pork. To create a low-fat version, I make the baskets from baked Chinese ravioli wrappers instead of the traditional deep-fried batter. You get the same audible crispness and explosive flavors with dramatically less fat and labor. The traditional golden basket has sloping, fluted sides—an effect you can achieve using miniature brioche molds. Otherwise, use small muffin tins. You will need 16 molds measuring 1 ½ to 2 inches across.

Asian sesame oil or spray oil
16 3- to 4-inch round Chinese ravioli
   wrappers

FOR THE FILLING:
12 ounces boneless, skinless chicken breast
2 teaspoons canola oil
3 cloves garlic, minced
2 shallots, minced (3 to 4 tablespoons)
1 tablespoon minced fresh ginger
1 to 3 jalapeño or other hot chilies, seeded
   and minced (optional)

2 teaspoons curry powder
2 tablespoons packed light-brown sugar,
   or to taste
2 tablespoons fish sauce (see page 25)
   or soy sauce, or to taste

FOR THE GARNISH:
1 cucumber, peeled, seeded, and cut into the
   finest possible dice
1 red bell pepper, cored, seeded,
   and minced
Cilantro sprigs (optional)

1. Preheat the oven to 375° F. Brush or spray the molds with the sesame or spray oil, and press a ravioli wrapper into each mold. Trim off any excess dough. Bake until the shells are browned and crisp, 10 to 15 minutes. Transfer the molds to a cooling rack.

2. While the shells are baking, prepare the filling: Trim any fat or sinew off the chicken breast. Mince the chicken with a cleaver, or cut

it into ½-inch cubes and grind it in a food processor. Heat the canola oil in a large non-stick frying pan set over medium-high heat. Add the garlic, shallots, ginger, chilies, and curry powder, and cook, stirring continuously, until lightly browned, about 3 minutes.

3. Add the chicken and sauté until cooked through, about 5 minutes, crumbling it with a wooden spoon. Add the sugar and fish sauce,

and cook 1 minute, or until the mixture is thick and flavorful. Correct the seasoning with fish sauce or sugar: the filling should be salty, sweet, and spicy. The recipe can be prepared ahead to this stage and refrigerated.

4. Just before serving, place 1 tablespoon of hot filling in each pastry shell. Garnish with a teaspoon each of the cucumber and bell pepper, and a cilantro sprig, if desired. Serve at once.

Makes 16 baskets

50 CALORIES PER PIECE; 4 G PROTEIN; 1.7 G FAT; 0.2 G SATURATED FAT; 5 G CARBOHYDRATE; 172 MG SODIUM; 11 MG CHOLESTEROL

BRAZILIAN STUFFED CRAB

Casquinha de siri (literally, "crab shells") turn up in seaside communities throughout Brazil, where tiny surf crabs are stuffed with a lively mixture of crabmeat, bell pepper, and chilies. If you live in a fishing town, you may be able to find tiny blue crab shells for stuffing; otherwise, use scallop shells, mussel shells, or small gratin dishes. You will need 16 shells. You could even use the stuffing for filling crepes (see page 23). This recipe can also be made with cooked shrimp instead of crabmeat.

1 tablespoon extra-virgin olive oil
½ large red onion, finely chopped
  (about ¾ cup)
2 cloves garlic, minced
½ green bell pepper, cored, seeded, and
  finely chopped
1 to 2 jalapeños or other hot chilies, seeded
  and minced (for a hotter stuffing leave in
  the seeds)
1 pound lump crabmeat
1 small tomato, peeled, seeded, and diced
  (see page xiv)

2 tablespoons flour
1 cup skim milk (see Note)
3 tablespoons finely chopped cilantro or
  parsley (preferably flat-leaf)
2 teaspoons fresh lime juice, or to taste
Salt and freshly ground black pepper
¼ cup dry bread crumbs
2 to 3 tablespoons grated fresh Parmesan
  cheese (preferably Parmigiano-Reggiano)

1. Heat the oil in a large nonstick frying pan set over medium heat. Add the onion, half the garlic, the bell pepper, and the chile, and cook until soft and just beginning to brown, about 5 minutes. Meanwhile, pick through the crabmeat to remove any bits of shell.

2. Increase the heat to high and add the tomato and crab. Cook until the liquid evaporates, about 1 minute. Stir in the flour and cook

1 minute. Stir in the milk and bring to a boil. Reduce the heat and gently simmer until thick, about 2 minutes. Remove the pan from the heat and stir in the cilantro and lime juice. Season with salt and pepper. Correct the seasoning with more lime juice if needed: the stuffing should be highly seasoned.

3. Fill the shells with the stuffing. Sprinkle with bread crumbs and grated cheese. The

recipe can be prepared ahead to this stage and refrigerated.

4. Preheat the oven to 400° F. Just before serving, bake the stuffed crab shells on a baking sheet until the top is crusty and brown and the filling is bubbling hot, about 10 minutes.

Note: For a more authentic flavor, and if your fat budget allows, you could use lower-fat or reduced-fat coconut milk (one good brand is A Taste of Thai) in place of some or all of the skim milk.   *Makes 16 stuffed crabs*

39 CALORIES PER PIECE; 3 G PROTEIN; 1.3 G FAT; 0.3 G SATURATED FAT; 4 G CARBOHYDRATE; 111 MG SODIUM; 5 MG CHOLESTEROL

SHIITAKE-STUFFED MUSHROOMS

These stuffed mushroom caps are for people who really like mushrooms. The filling is made with finely chopped shiitake. If fresh shiitake are unavailable, you could substitute dried Chinese black mushrooms (soak 8 caps in warm water for 1 hour) or another type of exotic mushroom. For a real treat, use jumbo mushroom caps for stuffing.

24 medium white mushrooms or
  12 large mushrooms
Spray oil or oil for brushing
3½ ounces fresh shiitake mushrooms,
  stemmed and quartered
1 tablespoon extra-virgin olive oil
2 to 3 shallots, minced (about 6 tablespoons)
2 cloves garlic, minced

¼ cup minced fresh parsley
  (preferably flat-leaf)
1 teaspoon sweet paprika, plus more as
  needed and for garnish
⅓ cup nonfat sour cream, plus
  1 to 2 tablespoons for garnish
Salt and freshly ground black pepper

1. Trim the dirty ends of the white mushroom stems and discard. Using a melon baller or grapefruit spoon, remove the stems and reserve. Spray or brush a baking dish with oil and arrange the mushroom caps on the dish, stem side up.

2. Finely chop the shiitake and the mushroom stems in a food processor or by hand. Heat the olive oil in a large nonstick frying pan set over high heat. Add the shallots and garlic and cook until translucent and fragrant, about 1 minute. Lower the heat to medium and stir in the chopped mushrooms. Cook until most of the liquid evaporates, about 5 minutes. Stir in

the parsley, paprika, and sour cream, season with salt and pepper, and simmer 2 minutes. Correct the seasoning with salt or paprika: the filling should be highly seasoned.

3. Spoon the filling into the mushroom caps. Place a dab of sour cream on top of each mushroom (or squirt thin squiggles from a squirt bottle) and sprinkle with paprika. The mushroom caps can be prepared up to 6 hours ahead to this stage and refrigerated.

4. Preheat the oven to 400° F. Bake the mushroom caps until they are soft and browned, about 15 minutes. Transfer to a platter and serve at once.

Note: To make mushroom crepes, finely chop the mushroom caps as well as the stems and use the mixture to fill crepes (see page 23).

Makes 24 medium stuffed mushrooms or 12 large

14 CALORIES PER PIECE; 0.5 G PROTEIN; 0.7 G FAT; 0.1 G SATURATED FAT; 2 G CARBOHYDRATE; 8 MG SODIUM; 0 MG CHOLESTEROL

OYSTERS ON THE HALF SHELL WITH MANGO MIGNONETTE

I love oysters on the half shell, especially when served with the zestily tart French dipping sauce, mignonette. The term (literally, "little darling") refers to cracked black peppercorns. (To crack peppercorns, coarsely crush in a mortar and pestle or wrap in a dish towel and smash under the edge of a heavy frying pan.) Mango adds a tropical touch to a French classic.

FOR THE MIGNONETTE SAUCE:
2 to 3 large shallots (6 tablespoons minced)
½ ripe mango, peeled, seeded, and cut into
¼-inch dice (6 tablespoons minced)
1 tablespoon cracked black peppercorns

½ cup red or white wine vinegar
½ cup dry white wine
salt

24 oysters in the shells

1. Combine the ingredients for the mignonette sauce in a mixing bowl and stir to mix, adding salt to taste.

2. Just before serving, shuck the oysters. (It's a good idea to wear heavy gloves to protect your hands while shucking.) Arrange the oysters on a platter lined with ice or seaweed or both. Spoon a little Mango Mignonette sauce over each oyster and serve the remainder on the side, in a bowl with a spoon.   *Makes 24 pieces*

28 CALORIES PER PIECE; 2.8 G PROTEIN; 0.7 G FAT; 0.2 G SATURATED FAT; 3 G CARBOHYDRATE; 31 MG SODIUM; 14 MG CHOLESTEROL

ON A SKEWER

SATÉ MIXED GRILL WITH SPICY PEANUT SAUCE

Satés (pronounced "sah-TAYS") are bite-size kebabs enjoyed throughout Southeast Asia.
I've omitted the fat-laden coconut milk used in traditional recipes and added spices, lime juice,
and fish sauce for flavor. If fish sauce is unavailable, you can substitute soy sauce.

½ pound skinless, boneless chicken breast
½ pound lean pork, such as loin or tenderloin
½ pound lean beef, such as sirloin or
  tenderloin
½ pound medium shrimp

FOR THE MARINADE:
⅓ cup fish sauce (see Note on page 25)
  or soy sauce

⅓ cup fresh lime juice
¼ cup honey
4 cloves garlic, minced
2 teaspoons ground coriander
2 teaspoons ground turmeric

Spicy Peanut Sauce (recipe follows)
About 40 6-inch bamboo skewers

1. Wash and dry the chicken, pork, and beef, and trim off any fat or sinew. Cut the chicken and pork into strips about 3 inches long and ½ inch wide. Slice the beef into long, thin strips.

Peel and devein the shrimp. Put each ingredient in a separate nonreactive bowl.

2. Make the marinade: Put the fish sauce, lime juice, honey, garlic, coriander, and tur-

Beef Saté
Yakitori
Chicken Saté
Seville Saté
Shrimp Saté

49

meric in a nonreactive mixing bowl and stir to combine. Divide the marinade among the four bowls of ingredients and marinate 30 minutes. Meanwhile, soak the skewers in cold water.

3. Preheat a grill or broiler to high. Thread the chicken, pork, beef, and shrimp onto the skewers (10 skewers of each ingredient). Grill or broil the satés until cooked through, about 1 to 3 minutes per side. If the skewer ends begin to burn, protect them with strips of aluminum foil.

4. Transfer the satés to a platter and serve with Spicy Peanut Sauce.   *Makes 40 kebabs*

33 CALORIES PER PIECE; 4 G PROTEIN; 0.7 G FAT; 0.3 G SATURATED FAT; 2.2 G CARBOHYDRATE; 189 MG SODIUM; 18 MG CHOLESTEROL

SPICY PEANUT SAUCE

Peanut sauce is the traditional accompaniment to satés. I've lightened the recipe by reducing the amount of peanut butter and replacing the coconut milk with chicken stock.

⅔ cup warm chicken or vegetable stock
⅓ cup chunky peanut butter
3 tablespoons fish sauce or soy sauce, or to taste (see Note, page 25)
3 tablespoons fresh lime juice, or to taste
1 tablespoon honey
1 ripe tomato, peeled, seeded, and chopped (about ¾ cup) (see page xiv)

4 scallions, trimmed and minced
2 cloves garlic, minced
1 tablespoon minced fresh ginger
1 to 3 jalapeño chilies, seeded and minced (for a hotter sauce, leave in the seeds)
¼ cup finely chopped fresh cilantro, plus sprigs for garnish

1. Put the stock, peanut butter, fish sauce, lime juice, honey, tomato, scallion, garlic, ginger, chilies, and cilantro in a nonreactive saucepan and bring to a boil. Reduce the heat and

simmer, whisking, until the sauce is thick and creamy, about 2 minutes.

2. Correct the seasoning with fish sauce, lime juice, or honey: the sauce should be salty, tart, and sweet. Transfer the sauce to bowls and garnish with sprigs of cilantro.

Makes about 1½ cups

17 CALORIES PER SERVING; 0.7 G PROTEIN; 1.1 G FAT; 0.2 G SATURATED FAT; 1.4 G CARBOHYDRATE; 108 MG SODIUM; 0 MG CHOLESTEROL

Yakitori (Chicken and Scallion Kebabs)

*Yakitori—tiny chicken-and-scallion kebabs basted with teriyaki sauce—is a popular Japanese appetizer.
Replacing the traditional sugar with maple syrup adds more flavor. Traditionally, yakitori is cooked
on a hibachi; it can also be cooked on a barbecue grill or under the broiler.*

1 pound boneless, skinless chicken breast
1 bunch large scallions

FOR THE MARINADE:
3 tablespoons soy sauce
3 tablespoons maple syrup
3 tablespoons mirin (see Note)
1 teaspoon Asian sesame oil

2 scallions, trimmed and finely chopped
2 cloves garlic, minced
2 teaspoons minced fresh ginger
1½ teaspoons black or toasted white sesame
    seeds, for garnish (see Note)

12 6-inch bamboo skewers

1. Wash and dry the chicken and trim off any fat or sinew. Cut the chicken into pieces 1 inch long and ½ inch wide. Trim the roots off the scallions. Cut the white parts into 1-inch pieces and the green parts into 2-inch pieces.

2. Make the marinade: Put the soy sauce, maple syrup, mirin, sesame oil, scallion, garlic, and ginger in a mixing bowl and stir to combine. Add the chicken and marinate 30 minutes. Meanwhile, soak the skewers in cold water.

3. Preheat the hibachi, grill, or broiler to high. Thread the chicken and scallion pieces crosswise onto the skewers, alternating them. Fold the scallion greens in half before skewering. Reserve any excess marinade.

4. Grill or broil the yakitori until cooked through, 1 to 2 minutes per side, basting with the remaining marinade. If the skewer ends begin to burn, protect them with strips of aluminum foil. Sprinkle the kebabs with sesame seeds and serve at once.

Note: Mirin is a Japanese sweet rice wine used for cooking. Look for it in Japanese and natural foods markets and many supermarkets. You can substitute sake, cream sherry, or white wine sweetened with a little sugar or honey. Black sesame seeds are available at Japanese markets and natural foods stores. To toast sesame seeds, cook in a dry frying pan over medium heat until golden brown, 3 to 5 minutes.

Makes 12 kebabs, which will serve 4 to 6

55 CALORIES PER SERVING; 6 G PROTEIN; 1 G FAT; 0.2 G SATURATED FAT; 4 G CARBOHYDRATE; 271 MG SODIUM; 15 MG CHOLESTEROL

SEVILLE "SATÉ"

This dish, marinated in paprika, sherry, and sherry vinegar, has a decidedly Spanish accent.
It is, in fact, a popular Spanish tapas.

1 pound lean pork loin or tenderloin
36 pearl onions

FOR THE MARINADE:
1 small onion, diced (about ¾ cup)
4 cloves garlic, minced
3 tablespoons minced parsley
   (preferably flat-leaf)
1 tablespoon Spanish paprika or Hungarian
   sweet paprika
½ teaspoon hot-pepper flakes

½ teaspoon ground cumin
½ teaspoon dried oregano
¼ teaspoon saffron threads
2 tablespoons sherry vinegar or
   red-wine vinegar
2 tablespoons dry sherry
2 teaspoons extra-virgin olive oil
Salt and freshly ground black pepper

16 6-inch bamboo skewers

1. Trim any fat or sinew off the pork and cut it into ¾-inch cubes. Peel the pearl onions. Cook the onions in 1 quart boiling salted water until just tender, about 2 minutes. Drain the onions, rinse under cold water, and drain again.

2. Make the marinade: Put the diced onion, garlic, parsley, paprika, hot-pepper flakes, cumin, oregano, saffron, vinegar, sherry, and oil in a nonreactive mixing bowl, season with salt and pepper, and stir to combine. Add the pork and pearl onions and marinate 1 hour. Meanwhile, soak the skewers in cold water.

3. Preheat a grill or broiler to high. Thread the pork onto the skewers, alternating with pearl onions. Grill until the pork is cooked, 1 to 2 minutes per side, basting with any remaining marinade. If the ends begin to burn, protect them with strips of aluminum foil. Serve at once.

Makes 16 kebabs

59 CALORIES PER PIECE; 7 G PROTEIN; 1.7 G FAT; 0.5 G SATURATED FAT; 4 G CARBOHYDRATE; 17 MG SODIUM; 20 MG CHOLESTEROL

PERSIAN SHRIMP KEBABS WITH POMEGRANATE DIP

Yogurt, onions, lemon, and saffron are some of the defining flavors of Persian cooking. Iranians combine these to make a tangy marinade for grilled fare of all sorts. The pomegranate dip isn't particularly traditional, but pomegranate syrup (sometimes called pomegranate molasses) is a popular ingredient in the Near East.

24 large shrimp (1 to 1½ pounds)
1 small onion

FOR THE MARINADE:
½ teaspoon saffron threads
2 teaspoons warm water
1 cup nonfat plain yogurt
¼ cup fresh lemon juice
1 medium onion, thinly sliced
Salt and freshly ground black pepper

FOR THE SAUCE:
1 cup nonfat yogurt
2 tablespoons pomegranate syrup (see Note)
1 tablespoon minced fresh dill or cilantro
½ teaspoon ground coriander
1 clove garlic, minced

12 6-inch bamboo skewers

1. Peel and devein the shrimp. Peel the onion and cut it in half crosswise. Cut each half into 6 wedges.

2. Make the marinade: Put the saffron in a nonreactive mixing bowl and pulverize it with the end of a wooden spoon. Add the water and let stand 3 minutes. Stir in the yogurt, lemon juice, and sliced onion, and season with salt and pepper. Add the shrimp and marinate 30 to 60 minutes. Meanwhile, soak the skewers in cold water.

3. Make the sauce: Put the yogurt, pome-

granate syrup, dill, ground coriander, and garlic in a mixing bowl, and season with salt and pepper: the mixture should be highly seasoned. Transfer the sauce to a serving bowl or ramekin.

4. Preheat the grill or broiler to high. Thread the shrimp onto the skewers, 2 shrimp to a skewer, with an onion wedge between them. Grill the kebabs until the shrimp is cooked, about 1 minute per side. If the skewer ends begin to burn, protect them with strips of aluminum foil. Arrange the kebabs on a platter and serve with the sauce for dipping.

Note: Look for pomegranate syrup at Middle Eastern and Iranian markets. If it is not available in your area, substitute balsamic vinegar syrup, made by boiling down ½ cup balsamic vinegar to 2 tablespoons.   *Makes 12 kebabs*

72 CALORIES PER KEBAB; 9 G PROTEIN; 0.4 G FAT; 0.1 G SATURATED FAT; 8 G CARBOHYDRATE; 98 MG SODIUM; 59 MG CHOLESTEROL

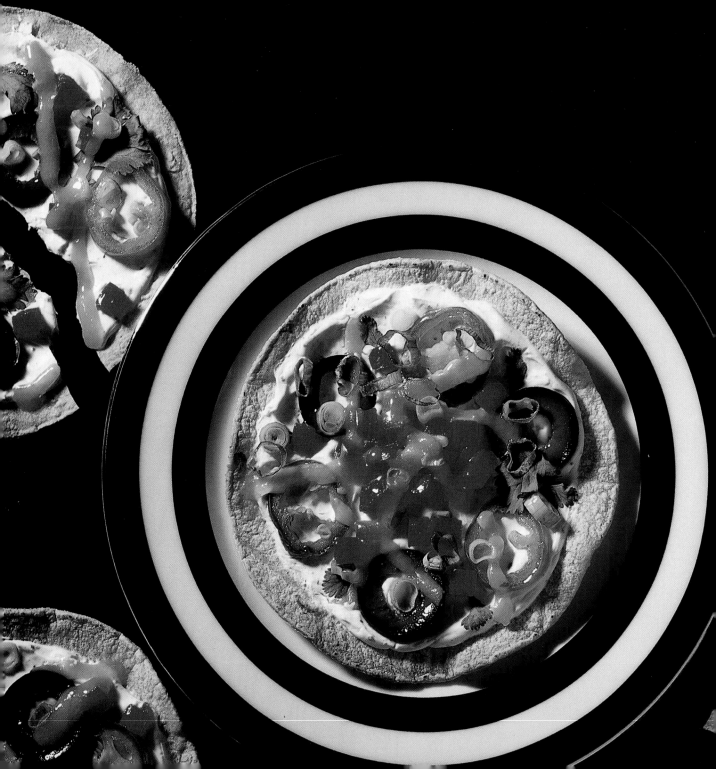

On a Canapé

Nacho Pizzettas

This dish combines two favorite American snacks, nachos and pizza.
Feel free to vary the toppings to suit your taste. The recipe can be doubled or tripled.

12 4½-inch corn tortillas
1 cup nonfat sour cream
½ teaspoon ground cumin
Salt and freshly ground black pepper
1 ripe tomato, seeded and cut into
   ¼-inch dice (see page xiv)
6 to 8 pitted black olives, thinly sliced

6 to 8 drained pickled jalapeño peppers,
   thinly sliced
4 scallions, trimmed and thinly sliced
½ cup cilantro sprigs
1½ ounces sharp cheddar cheese,
   shredded (about ½ cup)

1. Preheat the oven to 350° F. Arrange the tortillas on baking sheets and bake until crisp and just beginning to brown, about 10 minutes. Transfer the tortillas to wire racks.

2. Meanwhile, put the sour cream and cumin in a mixing bowl, and whisk to combine. Season with salt and pepper: the mixture should be highly seasoned.

3. Preheat the broiler. Arrange the tortillas on the baking sheets. Spread a little of the sour-cream mixture on each pizzetta. Sprinkle with the tomato, olive, jalapeño, scallion, cilantro, and grated cheese. Broil the pizzettas until the cheese melts and the topping is hot, about 2 minutes. Transfer to a platter and serve at once. *Makes 12 pizzettas*

81 CALORIES PER PIECE; 3.5 G PROTEIN; 2.7 G FAT; 1.1 G SATURATED FAT; 4 G CARBOHYDRATE; 141 MG SODIUM; 5 MG CHOLESTEROL

BRUSCHETTE WITH THREE TOPPINGS

Bruschetta (pronounced broo-SKEH-tah) is an Italian canapé, a grilled bread slice traditionally rubbed with garlic and drizzled with olive oil, today often topped with a simple salad or pâté. Grilling gives the bread a distinctive smoky flavor, but you can also toast the bread under the broiler. This recipe makes enough bruschette for one of the following toppings, or for a third of a batch of each.

1 2-inch-wide French bread or 3-inch-wide
  Italian bread
1 to 2 tablespoons olive oil (optional)
1 clove garlic, peeled and halved

Tomato and Arugula Topping (see page 59)
Charred-Pepper Topping (see page 60)
Roasted Mushroom Topping (see page 61)

1. Preheat the grill or broiler to medium. Cut the bread into ½-inch-thick slices. If you are using French bread, cut the slices on the diagonal. Lightly brush each slice with olive oil.

2. Grill or broil the bread 1 to 2 minutes per side, or until nicely browned. Transfer to a wire rack.

3. Rub each bruschetta with the cut side of the garlic. Place a heaping tablespoon of Tomato and Arugula Topping, Charred-Pepper Topping, or Roasted Mushroom Topping on each. *Makes about 40 pieces*

31 CALORIES PER PIECE; 1 G PROTEIN; 0.4 G FAT; 0.1 G SATURATED FAT; 6 G CARBOHYDRATE; 63 MG SODIUM; 0 MG CHOLESTEROL

TOMATO AND ARUGULA TOPPING

I like to think of this colorful topping as Italian salsa. You can have the ingredients ready,
but don't combine them more than 20 minutes before serving—this is best when freshly made.

3 ripe tomatoes, peeled
1 bunch arugula, washed and cut crosswise
   into ¼-inch slivers
2 to 3 shallots, minced (about 3 tablespoons)
1 clove garlic, minced

1 tablespoon drained capers
1½ tablespoons balsamic vinegar, or to taste
1½ tablespoons extra-virgin olive oil
Salt and freshly ground black pepper

1. Set a strainer over a nonreactive bowl and seed the tomatoes over it, reserving the juices. Cut the tomatoes into ¼-inch dice.

2. Put the tomato, arugula, shallots, garlic, capers, vinegar, and oil in a nonreactive mixing bowl. Add enough of the reserved tomato liquid to make a mixture that is moist but not wet. Season with salt and pepper, and stir to combine. Correct the seasoning with vinegar or salt.

Makes about 2½ cups

8 CALORIES PER SERVING; 0.1 G PROTEIN; 0.5 G FAT; 0.1 G SATURATED FAT; 0.8 G CARBOHYDRATE; 6 MG SODIUM; 0 MG CHOLESTEROL

CHARRED-PEPPER TOPPING

This is the one dish you can get away with burning! Charring imparts a wonderful smoky flavor to peppers.
I like to use a combination of red, yellow, and green peppers, but any color will do.

3 bell peppers
1 tablespoon extra-virgin olive oil
1 tablespoon red-wine vinegar, or to taste

1 clove garlic, minced
1 teaspoon dried oregano
Salt and freshly ground black pepper

1. Char the peppers on all sides by placing them directly on top of a gas or electric burner heated to high. Turn the pepper with tongs to ensure even charring. (You can also char the peppers on the barbecue or under the broiler.) The charring should take 6 to 8 minutes.

2. Place the charred peppers in a deep bowl and cover with plastic wrap or a plate, or place peppers in a sealed paper bag until cool. (The resulting steam will loosen the skins.) Transfer the peppers to a cutting board and scrape off the skin with a paring knife. Cut each pepper in half. Core, seed, and finely dice the peppers, reserving any juices.

3. Place the peppers in a nonreactive mixing bowl and stir in the pepper juices, oil, vinegar, garlic, and oregano. Season with salt and pepper. Correct the seasoning with vinegar or salt.

Makes about 2 ½ cups

5 CALORIES PER SERVING; 0.1 G PROTEIN; 0.4 G FAT; 0.1 G SATURATED FAT; 0.4 G CARBOHYDRATE; 0 MG SODIUM; 0 MG CHOLESTEROL

ROASTED MUSHROOM TOPPING

High-heat roasting is a great way to bring out the flavor of vegetables, with very little fat. You can use any type of mushroom for this recipe, from commonplace button mushrooms to shiitakes or porcini. Better still, use a mixture.

1½ to 2 pounds mushrooms, trimmed
5 to 6 shallots, thinly sliced (about 5 ounces)
6 cloves garlic, minced
2 tablespoons chopped fresh dill (or other fresh herb), plus dill sprigs for garnish

2 tablespoons extra-virgin olive oil
Salt and freshly ground black pepper
¾ cup no-fat sour cream

1. Preheat the oven to 450° F. Quarter the large mushrooms, cut the mediums in half, and leave the small ones whole. Place the mushrooms, shallots, garlic, half the dill, and the oil, salt, and pepper in a roasting pan and toss to mix.

2. Roast the mushrooms until nicely browned, 20 to 30 minutes, stirring often to coat with oil.

Do not overcook, or the mushrooms will become watery. Remove the pan from the oven and stir in the remaining dill and the sour cream. Correct the seasoning as needed.

3. Spoon the mushrooms onto the bruschette. Garnish with sprigs of dill.

Makes about 2 ½ cups

16 CALORIES PER SERVING; 0.7 G PROTEIN; 0.8 G FAT; 0.1 G SATURATED FAT; 1.8 G CARBOHYDRATE; 8 MG SODIUM; 0 MG CHOLESTEROL

GALLOPING HORSES (SPICED PORK ON PINEAPPLE)

I first learned of this colorfully named hors d'oeuvre from Nancy MacDermott, former Peace Corps worker, Thai cooking authority extraordinaire, and author of one of my favorite Thai cookbooks, Real Thai. *The combination of fruit and meat, sweet and salty, is a hallmark of Thai cooking, and these pineapple wedges topped with spiced pork are as refreshing as they are unusual. When buying pineapples, look for a gold rather than a green skin: this indicates a riper, sweeter pineapple.*

½ ripe pineapple (cut lengthwise)

FOR THE TOPPING:
8 to 10 ounces lean pork, such as tenderloin
   or center-cut boneless chops
1 tablespoon canola oil
2 cloves garlic, minced
2 shallots, minced
1 tablespoon minced fresh ginger
1 to 4 jalapeño or other hot chilies, seeded
   and minced (for a spicier topping,
   leave in the seeds)

1 teaspoon minced cilantro root (optional)
   (see Note)
3 tablespoons finely chopped fresh cilantro
2 tablespoons packed dark brown sugar
2 tablespoons fish sauce (see page 25)
   or soy sauce

FOR THE GARNISH:
1 to 2 tablespoons chopped unsalted dry-
   roasted peanuts
About 30 cilantro sprigs

1. Peel and core the pineapple. Cut the pineapple crosswise into ½-inch-thick rings, and cut each slice into 6 wedges. Arrange the pineapple pieces on a serving platter.

2. Trim any fat or sinew from the pork and mince it with a cleaver, or cut it into ½-inch cubes and grind it in a food processor. Heat the oil in a wok or a large frying pan (preferably nonstick) set over medium heat. Add the garlic,

shallots, ginger, chilies, and cilantro root, and stir-fry until lightly browned, about 2 minutes.

3. Add the pork and stir-fry until cooked, about 3 minutes. Stir in the cilantro leaves, sugar, and fish sauce, and cook 1 minute. Correct the seasoning with fish sauce or sugar: the mixture should be sweet, salty, and a little spicy. Let the pork cool to room temperature. The recipe can be made ahead to this point and re-

frigerated. If this is done, let the dish come to room temperature before serving.

4. Mound a spoonful of the pork mixture on top of each pineapple wedge. Sprinkle with a little chopped peanut and garnish with a sprig of cilantro. Serve at once.

Note: The root of the cilantro plant is a popular Thai seasoning, with an aromatic, cilantro-like pungency and an earthy flavor reminiscent of celeriac or parsley root. Asian and Hispanic markets sell cilantro with the roots attached, and so do many gourmet shops and greengrocers. But don't worry if you can't find it—the Galloping Horses will be perfectly tasty without it. The topping can also be made with chicken breast or shrimp (10 ounces of shrimp in shells; 8 ounces of shelled shrimp). This recipe can be doubled or tripled to serve a larger crowd.

Makes about 30 pieces

24 CALORIES PER PIECE; 1.9 G PROTEIN; 0.9 G FAT; 0.2 G SATURATED FAT; 2.2 G CARBOHYDRATE; 94 MG SODIUM; 5 MG CHOLESTEROL

SMOKED TROUT MOUSSE ON CUCUMBER

Here's a handsome and refreshing canapé featuring smoked trout mousse on cucumber slices. Smoked trout is available at fish stores, gourmet shops, and many supermarkets. One excellent mail-order source is DuckTrap River Farm in Maine (telephone 800-828-3825). You could also prepare the recipe with smoked salmon or other smoked fish.

1 large English (hothouse) cucumber
1 smoked trout (8 to 10 ounces)
6 ounces low- or no-fat cream cheese,
  at room temperature

2 to 3 teaspoons prepared white horseradish
  (optional)
Salt and freshly ground black pepper
Dill sprigs, for garnish

1. Peel the cucumber, leaving narrow strips of peel to create a striped effect. Cut the cucumber into ¼-inch-thick slices. Blot the slices dry with paper towels and arrange them on a serving platter.

2. Prepare the trout mousse. Skin the trout and remove the meat from the bones with a fork. Purée the trout in a food processor. Add the cream cheese and process to a smooth paste. Add the horseradish and season with pepper and, if needed, salt. Transfer the mixture to a pastry bag fitted with a large star tip. Pipe rosettes of trout mousse onto the cucumber slices. Garnish each with a dill sprig.

Makes 48 pieces

16 CALORIES PER PIECE; 1.7 G PROTEIN; 0.8 G FAT; 0.8 G SATURATED FAT; 0.6 G CARBOHYDRATE; 22 MG SODIUM; 5 MG CHOLESTEROL

A New Shrimp Toast

Remember shrimp toast? The oily, deep-fried, but oh-so-luscious appetizer from the Cantonese restaurants of our childhood? Here's a heart-healthy version that is broiled instead of fried. The idea comes from Joyce Jue, author of the excellent book Asian Appetizers.

8-ounce can water chestnuts, drained
1 pound shrimp, peeled and deveined
   (1¼ pounds in shells)
3 cloves garlic, minced
4 scallions, trimmed and minced
1 tablespoon minced fresh ginger
1 tablespoon Chinese or Japanese rice wine,
   or dry sherry
2 to 3 teaspoons sugar
1 to 2 teaspoon hot sauce (optional)
1 large egg white
Salt and freshly ground black pepper
1 long, slender French bread (baguette)
1 to 2 teaspoons Asian sesame oil
Spray oil

1. Finely chop the water chestnuts by hand or in a food processor and transfer to a mixing bowl. Coarsely chop the shrimp in the food processor. Add the garlic, scallion, ginger, wine, sugar, hot sauce, and egg white, and season with salt and pepper. Process briefly to mix. Add the shrimp mixture to the water chestnuts and stir to mix. Correct the seasoning with salt: the mixture should be highly seasoned. (To taste the mixture for seasoning without eating raw seafood, cook a tiny bit on the end of a spoon in boiling water.)

2. Preheat the oven to 400° F. Cut the bread on the diagonal into ½-inch-thick slices. Arrange the slices on a baking sheet and lightly spray both sides with oil. Bake until golden brown on both sides, about 6 minutes per side. Transfer the bread slices to a wire rack.

3. Preheat the broiler. Spread a generous tablespoon of the shrimp mixture on each slice of bread and brush with sesame oil or spray with spray oil. Broil the toasts until the shrimp mixture is puffed and golden brown on top and cooked through, 2 to 4 minutes.

Makes about 30 pieces

68 CALORIES PER PIECE; 5 G PROTEIN; 0.9 G FAT; 0.2 G SATURATED FAT; 9 G CARBOHYDRATE; 112 MG SODIUM; 26 MG CHOLESTEROL

IN A CRUST

PISSALADIÈRE (FRENCH ONION PIZZA)

This onion tart from Provence is one of my favorite savory pies. The anchovies and olives are arranged in a lattice pattern to make a stunning presentation. Note: You could also make 6 to 8 individual 4-inch pissaladières.

2 tablespoons extra-virgin olive oil
4 large onions, thinly sliced (7 to 8 cups)
4 cloves garlic, minced
3 tablespoons chopped fresh mixed herbs, such as basil, rosemary, and parsley (preferably flat-leaf)
¼ teaspoon cayenne pepper
Salt and freshly ground black pepper

1 recipe Basic Pizza Dough, prepared through step 3 (see page 72)
3 ripe tomatoes, thinly sliced
2 2-ounce cans anchovy fillets, drained and patted dry
½ cup oil- or brine-cured black olives

Spray oil

1. Preheat the oven to 375° F. Heat the olive oil in 1 large or 2 medium nonstick frying pans set over medium heat. Add the onions and garlic and cook until very soft, nicely browned, and caramelized, 10 to 15 minutes, stirring often. Lower the heat if the onions start to burn. Stir in the herbs and cayenne, and season with salt and pepper: the mixture should be highly seasoned. Let the mixture cool slightly.

2. Meanwhile, roll out the dough, stretching it as you roll, and use it to line a 12-inch tart pan with fluted sides and a removable bottom. Spread the onion mixture over the dough and arrange the tomato slices on top of it. Cut the anchovies in half lengthwise. Arrange half the anchovies in parallel rows, 1 inch apart, on top of the tomatoes. Turn the pissaladière 60 degrees and arrange the remaining anchovies in parallel rows to form a neat lattice. Place a whole or half olive in the center of each dia-

mond formed by the lattice. Lightly spray the top of the pissaladière with oil. Let the pissaladière stand 15 minutes while the dough rises.

3. Bake the pissaladière until the tomatoes are soft and the edges of the crust are nicely browned, 40 to 50 minutes. Remove the sides of the pan and cut the pissaladière into wedges or squares. It's equally delicious served hot or at room temperature.

Makes 1 12-inch pizza, which will serve 8 to 10

340 CALORIES PER SERVING; 12 G PROTEIN; 9 G FAT; 1.3 G SATURATED FAT; 55 G CARBOHYDRATE; 1,209 MG SODIUM; 12 MG CHOLESTEROL

RED-ONION AND ROSEMARY FOCACCIA

Thicker than pizza but flatter than a conventional loaf, the Italian bread known as focaccia
(pronounced "foh-KAH-cha") has become a North American favorite.
A dark-colored baking pan will give you a crisper, browner crust.

1 envelope dry yeast
2 teaspoons sugar
1½ cups warm (90° F.) water
2 teaspoons salt
3 teaspoons extra-virgin olive oil
4½ to 5 cups unbleached white flour

Spray oil
Coarse cornmeal
1 small red onion, thinly sliced
2 teaspoons chopped fresh or dried rosemary
Kosher salt and freshly cracked or coarsely
    ground black pepper

1. Combine the yeast, sugar, and ¼ cup of the water in a large mixing bowl. Let stand until foamy, about 10 minutes. (If yeast does not foam, discard it and start over.)

2. Stir in the remaining 1¼ cups water, the 2 teaspoons salt, and 1½ teaspoons of the olive oil. Stir in the flour ½ cup at a time to form a soft, pliable dough that comes away from the sides of the bowl. Turn the dough out onto a lightly floured work surface and knead it until it is smooth and elastic, 6 to 8 minutes, adding more flour as necessary.

3. Spray a large mixing bowl with oil. Put the dough in the bowl and cover with plastic wrap. Let rise in a warm, draft-free place until doubled in bulk, 1 to 2 hours.

4. Punch down the dough and roll it out ½ inch thick into an 11 × 17-inch rectangle, stretching it as you roll. Sprinkle a nonstick baking sheet with cornmeal. Transfer the focaccia to the baking sheet and cover with a clean cloth. Let rise until doubled in height, 30 to 60 minutes.

5. Preheat the oven to 375° F. Poke your fingers all over the surface of the focaccia to decoratively dimple the surface. Arrange the onion slices on top. Brush with the remaining 1½ teaspoons olive oil and sprinkle with the rosemary, kosher salt, and cracked pepper.

6. Bake the focaccia until crisp and golden brown, 20 to 30 minutes. Let cool slightly before serving. Cut into squares or rectangles and serve.

Note: The dough can also be made in a mixer with a dough hook or a food processor. (If using the latter, let the yeast, sugar, and water foam in a small bowl. Place the flour and salt in the processor bowl. Add the yeast mixture, remaining water, and olive oil. Knead the dough by pulsing the machine in bursts.)

Makes 1 11 × 17-inch focaccia,
which will serve 8 to 10

291 CALORIES PER SERVING; 8 G PROTEIN; 2 G FAT; 0.4 G SATURATED FAT; 58 G CARBOHYDRATE; 535 MG SODIUM; 0 MG CHOLESTEROL

TOMATO AND ARUGULA PIZZA

Wafer-thin and crackling crisp are the pizzas prepared by my friend Mark Militello, the owner-chef of Mark's Place,
Mark's Las Olas, and Mark's in the Grove in south Florida. They shatter into a thousand savory shards
when you bite into them. This pizza, topped with caramelized onions and a tomato-and-arugula salad,
offers an interesting contrast of temperatures, textures, and flavors.

2 tablespoons extra-virgin olive oil
1 medium red onion, thinly sliced
3 ounces shiitake mushrooms, stemmed and
   thinly sliced
Salt and freshly ground black pepper
1 recipe Basic Pizza Dough, prepared through
   step 3 (see page 72)

½ cup low- or no-fat tomato sauce (optional)
   (see Note)
1 bunch arugula, stems removed
1 ripe tomato, seeded and cut into
   ½-inch dice
2 teaspoons balsamic vinegar, or to taste

1. Preheat the oven to 450° F. Heat 1 tablespoon of the oil in a large nonstick frying pan set over medium heat. Add the onion and cook 5 minutes, stirring often. Add the shiitakes and cook, stirring, 5 minutes more, or until the onions are nicely browned and caramelized. Season with salt and pepper.

2. Roll out the dough into an 11 × 17-inch rectangle, stretching it as you roll. Transfer it to a baking sheet and flute the edges. Bake 5 minutes. Cover with the tomato sauce and the onion mixture. Bake another 5 to 10 minutes, or until the crust is browned and crisp, about 10 minutes in all.

3. Meanwhile, toss the arugula and diced tomatoes with the remaining 1 tablespoon olive oil and the vinegar. Season with salt and pepper. When the pizza is cooked, pile the salad on top of the pizza. Cut the pizza into squares and serve immediately.

Note: Recipes for low- and no-fat tomato sauce can be found in my books *High-Flavor, Low-Fat Cooking*; *High-Flavor, Low-Fat Vegetarian Cooking*; and *High-Flavor, Low-Fat Pasta*.

Makes 1 11 × 17-inch pizza,
which will serve 8 to 10

231 CALORIES PER SERVING; 6 G PROTEIN; 4 G FAT; 0.6 G SATURATED FAT; 43 G CARBOHYDRATE; 406 MG SODIUM; 0 MG CHOLESTEROL

BASIC PIZZA DOUGH

Rye flour and honey give this pizza dough a rich, earthy flavor.

FOR THE STARTER:
1 teaspoon dry yeast
2 teaspoons honey
½ cup warm (90° F.) water
½ cup rye flour

TO FINISH THE DOUGH:
½ cup water

1 tablespoon skim milk
1 tablespoon extra-virgin olive oil (optional)
¼ cup rye flour
1½ tablespoons sugar
1½ teaspoons salt
2 cups bread flour, or all-purpose flour,
    plus more as needed
Spray oil

1. Prepare the starter: Combine the yeast, the honey, and the ½ cup warm water in a large mixing bowl. Let stand until foamy, about 10 minutes. (If yeast does not foam, discard it and start over.) Stir in the ½ cup rye flour and let rise 10 minutes.

2. Add the ½ cup water, skim milk, and olive oil, and stir to mix. Add the ¼ cup rye flour, the sugar, the salt, and enough bread flour to obtain a soft, pliable dough that comes away from the sides of the bowl.

3. Turn the dough out onto a lightly floured work surface and knead until smooth and elastic, about 5 minutes, adding more flour as necessary.

4. Spray a large mixing bowl with oil. Put the dough in the bowl and cover with plastic wrap. Let rise in a warm, draft-free place until doubled in bulk, 1 to 2 hours. Punch down the dough and roll it out to make pizzas, stretching it as you roll.

Note: The dough can also be made in a mixer with a dough hook or a food processor. (If using the latter, make the starter in a small mixing bowl. Place the flours, sugar, and salt in the processor bowl. Add the starter, ½ cup water, the milk, and the olive oil (if using). Knead the dough by pulsing the machine in bursts.)

Makes enough dough for 1 11 × 17-inch
rectangular pizza, 1 12-to-14-inch
round pizza, or 2 9-inch round pizzas

175 CALORIES PER SERVING; 5 G PROTEIN; 0.7 G FAT; 0.1 G SATURATED FAT; 36 G CARBOHYDRATE; 402 MG SODIUM; 0 MG CHOLESTEROL

TORTILLA ESPAÑOLA (SPANISH POTATO FRITTATA)

Tortillas are one of the national dishes of Spain. But don't envision a dish made with Mexican cornmeal flatcakes. In Spain tortilla *refers to an egg-and-potato dish—a sort of frittata or omelet served at tapas bars throughout the country. The bad news is that the traditional way to cook both the potatoes and the tortilla is by frying them in oceans of oil. To make my low-fat version, I roast the potatoes in the oven with garlic—lots of it. I replace some of the eggs with egg whites or egg substitute. Finally, I bake the tortilla in a bread-crumb-lined frying pan in the oven instead of frying it. The result is a moist, crusty Tortilla Española that's loaded with flavor.*

2 pounds potatoes (preferably Yukon Gold),
    peeled and quartered
1 to 2 tablespoons extra-virgin olive oil
Salt and freshly ground black pepper
1 to 2 heads garlic, broken into cloves
    and peeled

3 large eggs plus 6 large egg whites or
    1½ cups egg substitute
Spray oil
½ cup dry bread crumbs

1. Preheat the oven to 400° F. Place the potatoes in a roasting pan (preferably nonstick) just large enough to hold them in one layer. Toss with the olive oil and season with salt and pepper. Roast the potatoes 15 minutes. Add the garlic and continue roasting until the potatoes and garlic are soft, 30 to 40 minutes in all, stirring from time to time to keep the potatoes coated with oil. Remove the pan from the oven and reduce the heat to 350° F.

2. While the potatoes are cooking, put the eggs and egg whites in a large mixing bowl and whisk well. Spray a 9-inch ovenproof nonstick frying pan with oil. Add the bread crumbs and rotate the pan to coat the bottom and sides.

3. When the potatoes are cool enough to handle, cut them into ¼-inch slices. Stir the potatoes and garlic into the egg mixture. Correct the seasoning with salt and pepper: the mixture should be highly seasoned. Pour the mixture into the prepared frying pan. Smooth the surface of the tortilla with a fork, pressing down any pieces of protruding potato. Bake until the egg is set, about 20 minutes. Let cool 3 minutes. Place a round platter over the pan and invert the tortilla onto it. To serve, cut the tortilla into wedges or squares. The Spanish serve it either hot or at room temperature.

Makes 1 9-inch tortilla, which will serve 12

123 CALORIES PER SERVING; 5 G PROTEIN; 3 G FAT; 0.6 G SATURATED FAT; 19 G CARBOHYDRATE; 78 MG SODIUM; 53 MG CHOLESTEROL

INDEX